Shakespeare

Puritan and Recusant

By the
Rev. T. Carter

With a Prefatory Note by the
Rev. Principal J. Oswald Dykes, D.D.

AMS PRESS, INC.
NEW YORK

822.3
C

Reprinted from the edition of 1897, Edinburgh and London
First AMS EDITION published 1970
Manufactured in the United States of America

International Standard Book Number: 0-404-01397-X

Library of Congress Catalog Card Number: 70-129386

AMS PRESS, INC.
NEW YORK, N.Y. 10003

Shakespeare

Puritan and Recusant

To

The Countess of Warwick

*Whose ancestors rendered many and eminent
services to the Puritan cause
and whose gracious qualities have added
lustre to the honoured names of
" Brooke" and " Warwick"*

*This Book is
by her Ladyship's kind permission
dedicated with all respect*

Acknowledgment

*A word of acknowledgment of their uniform courtesy is
due to the Librarian and Officials of the
Birmingham Shakespeare Library*

Prefatory Note

THE lifetime of England's greatest poet covered a period, from 1564 to 1616, when the country was agitated from end to end by religious strife. In Hazlitt's words, "There was a mighty fermentation: the waters were out." When Shakespeare was born, the kingdom had just been passing through a series of revolutions in faith and worship, the most violent which it has ever sustained since its conversion to Christianity. During the whole of Elizabeth's reign the public mind was disturbed by the efforts of the Roman Catholic Church to recover through treasonable intrigue its lost ascendency. Meanwhile, the Reformed Church of England was settling down into the constitution, and shaping the formularies, which it still retains. But it was doing this amid the party strife of Churchmen. The prelatic majority was content to accept, even if reluctantly, the measure of reform which satisfied the Queen, and enjoyed in consequence the favour of the Government. But a minority of Churchmen, not inconsiderable either for numbers, for learning, or for social position, advocated a more thorough rejection of Catholic usages, and were driven by their conscientious scruples into recusancy or nonconformity.

Shakespeare was no recluse, but a man of the world, familiar with affairs, who led the busy life of a prosperous citizen. Yet of these heated contests going on around him between the old and the new Faiths, his plays and poems offer scarcely a trace. No critic has been able from his writings to infer with confidence to which side the poet's convictions inclined. It is a singular instance how the imaginative artist, moving in the elemental region of human passion, and breathing the serener air of poetic inspiration, may hold his art aloof from the storms which agitate his age.

Even from this seeming indifference to Church reform, as well as from the tone of his rare allusions to the party of change, Roman Catholic writers

Prefatory Note

have argued that Shakespeare's secret sympathies must have lain with the old Faith. Precarious at the best, this conclusion becomes more than doubtful if the argument of the present volume can be maintained. For it is the aim of my friend, Mr. Carter, in the following pages, to make it probable, from a re-examination of the data which we possess respecting the poet's father, that John Shakespeare of Stratford-on-Avon was not only no Papist, but an adherent of the most advanced section of Protestants.

To bestow on this party in the earlier years of the English Reformation the epithet of "Puritan," is to antedate, though only by a little, the introduction of that nickname. Curiously enough, the earliest instance of its employment occurs in the very year of the poet's birth. At that date, the friends of a more drastic reform, reinforced by the return from abroad of the Marian exiles, were on the point of advancing from the question of ceremonies and vestments, which in Henry's reign had been chiefly debated, to some deeper matters of Church discipline and polity which for a century to come were to divide English Churchmen into two camps. It was an advance which had important consequences; but it marked no change in the principles by which the party was guided. In substance the "harried" Puritans of Cartwright's school under Elizabeth and James represented the party which in a preceding reign had scrupled at sacerdotal vestments; just as in their turn Hooper and Latimer and Foxe had inherited the Lollard tradition of a still earlier generation. There is evidence indeed that the very name of "Lollard" lived on till it was exchanged in popular usage for the newer nickname of "Puritan," which took its place."[1]

If Mr. Carter's reading of the elder Shakespeare's life can be justified, the poet was at all events reared in a "Puritan" home. The presumption which would thence arise, that the aims of the advanced Protestants, as they commanded the sympathy of Shakespeare's earlier contemporary, Edmund Spenser, and claimed the powerful pen of his younger contemporary, John Milton, so they retained a hold on the mature intelligence of a

---

[1] See *Hist. MSS. Commission's Eleventh Report*, part vii. p. 253: "Discourse against profane Lollardes, commonly called Puritans.'

Prefatory Note 5

greater than either, is one which there is little or nothing that I know of in his writings to outweigh. Of course it must be left to the judgment of historical critics, and especially of Shakespearian students, to estimate the weight of the evidence on which Mr. Carter relies. But the point is one which, like everything bearing on the formation of Shakespeare's mind, has interest for all educated Englishmen. Those who recognise in the advanced Protestants or early Puritans under the Tudors, the men who in their day embraced most faithfully the ideas of the new era, the men of freest thought and keenest sympathy with pure and true religion, will find the suggestion no less natural than welcome that William Shakespeare was the child of a Puritan and Bible-loving home. For many a day the Elizabethan Puritan shared with his successor under the Commonwealth in the odium and derision with which from the Restoration onwards party rancour delighted to load the memory of a great, though in the end unsuccessful, party. Recent historians have passed a more favourable judgment. "Among their ranks," says Mr. S. R. Gardiner, " were to be found some of the most learned men and the ablest preachers in England."[1] Among them were men who had drunk in Reformed teaching at the feet of scholars like Bucer at Cambridge and Peter Martyr at Oxford, and who kept up close relations with the leading Continental Reformers, with Bullinger, with Calvin, with Beza, and with A'Lasco. Their chief strength lay in the younger generation growing up in the Universities; at Cambridge especially, where Cartwright held the Lady Margaret Professorship of Divinity. Not only in Emmanuel College, founded in 1584 by Sir Walter Mildmay, with a Puritan for its first Master, but in older foundations as well, such as Trinity and St. John's, a large number of the younger Regents gave trouble to the authorities by overt acts of nonconformity. Nor did the policy in Church matters of the Queen and of her prelates commend itself to the wisest of her statesmen. The words of Mr. Mullingar sum up the facts with substantial correctness when he affirms: "Nearly all Elizabeth's ministers, Cecil, Leicester, Knolles, Bedford and Walsingham, had Puritanical sympathies and lent their party sub-

[1] *History of England*, 2nd ed. i. 21.

Prefatory Note

stantial aid."[1] It is more difficult to ascertain on sure evidence what measure of support the party enjoyed among the substantial middle classes to which Shakespeare belonged—the yeomen and well-to-do burghers. It is certain at least that Shakespeare's own county of Warwick was in this respect one of the most Puritan in England. If it be true that two-thirds of King James' first Parliament were of this way of thinking,[2] it is evident enough that the repressive measures of the great Queen had been successful merely in restraining the open resistance of the advanced or "Puritan" Protestants in the Church, but by no means in reconciling England to her ecclesiastical policy.

All this, of course, does not strengthen the probability that John Shakespeare of Stratford-on-Avon was a Puritan. That must be left to rest on its proper evidence, which it is the design of this volume to set forth. But if Mr. Carter's reading of the facts be accepted, it is of consequence to remember that the stream of influence which

---

[1] *Cambridge Characteristics in the Seventeenth Century*, 1867.
[2] *State Papers* (*Dom.*), vii. 2.

in that case must have told powerfully on the boyhood of the future dramatist, was no side current, still less a reactionary eddy in the religious life of England, but a genuine, deep, and healthful movement of the nation's life, running in the line of what was sanest, and noblest, and fullest of promise for the national character in the future. If it was in a Puritan household Shakespeare grew to manhood, then the reverent temper of such a home, its familiarity with Holy Writ, its spirit of freedom in opinion, its grave conscientiousness and loyalty to principle under the frown of authority in Church and State, were all elements worthy to enter into the poet's moral and intellectual structure. They will have to be reckoned with by those who would understand aright the later work done by the most imperial intellect of all time.

Contents

CHAP.		PAGE
I.	THE EARLIER YEARS OF JOHN SHAKESPEARE, PURITAN AND RECUSANT	11
II.	"QUEEN, PRELATIST, AND PURITAN AGAINST ROMAN CATHOLIC"	49
III.	THE ALLEGED POVERTY OF JOHN SHAKESPEARE	81
IV.	ACTIVE PERSECUTION OF PURITANS, AND JOHN SHAKESPEARE'S INCREASING DIFFICULTIES	109
V.	MARKED DOWN AS A PURITAN RECUSANT	133
VI.	WILLIAM SHAKESPEARE AND PURITAN INFLUENCES	171
	APPENDICES	199
	INDEX	205

I

The Earlier Years of John Shakespeare

CHAPTER I

THE EARLIER YEARS OF JOHN SHAKESPEARE, PURITAN AND RECUSANT

JOHN SHAKESPEARE, father of the poet, came into the town of Stratford, from the neighbouring village of Snitterfield, in the year 1551. He was then a young man of twenty. The times were stirring ones, for the Protector Somerset had fallen, and the Earl of Warwick, afterwards Duke of Northumberland, was taking the leading part in the Government of the day, and identifying himself most actively with those reformers in religion who took their theology from Calvin, Knox, and Bucer. Possibly owing to his influence with the King, letters of incorporation were granted by Edward VI. whereby Stratford borough became subject to the rule of a bailiff or chief magistrate, fourteen aldermen, and fourteen burgesses. But the following year saw Mary ascend the throne of England, and the Roman Catholic faith become once more the established religion of the realm. With many men in those days of ecclesiastical confusion and unrest, belief was too often a matter of convenience rather than of conviction, and multitudes of the people quietly changed their religion and obeyed the Queen. Reformers who were in earnest protested and went into exile. It has been accepted, without much proof, however, that John Shakespeare, although born in Protestantism, had become, and remained all his life, a staunch adherent and professor of the ancient Faith, and that, in the words of Carlyle, William Shakespeare "was the noblest product of Middle-Age Catholicism." There is, however, no documentary witness of this Roman Catholicism of John Shakespeare, and the evidence of his life points conclusively in an opposite direction, namely, to the steadfast section of the Protestant Reformation which afterwards became so widely known as the Puritan. In order to present this evidence as clearly as possible it will be necessary to follow somewhat carefully the record

Earlier Years of John Shakespeare 15

of John Shakespeare's life, and at the same time place him in his true religious environment and historical setting.

In the early years of his residence in the borough, business matters evidently absorbed all his attention, and the Stratford Records are principally of these. In 1556 he had made enough money to purchase one of the best dwellings in the town, the house in Henley Street annexed to that which is now shown as the birthplace, and another little property in Greenhill Street or More Towns End.

The record of the sale is in the legal Latin of the time, and runs as follows:— " Item, quod Edwardus West alienavit predicto Johanni Shakespere unum tenementum cum gardino adjacente in Henley Stret per redditum inde domino per annum vJd et sectam curie, et idem Johannes presens in curia fecit fidelitatem visus etc."

The next year, 1557, probably saw him bring a fair maiden to the house in Henley Street, for in the preceding autumn there had died at Wilmcote, three miles from Stratford, a country gentleman of worshipful descent named Robert Arden, whose youngest and favourite daughter, Mary, was betrothed to John Shakespeare. A fairly large inheritance had fallen to her by her father's death; and the reversion of two farmhouses at Snitterfield, with about one hundred acres of land, an estate at the Asbies, Wilmcote, of sixty acres, and a substantial pecuniary legacy would come as a welcome help to one whose rapidly increasing business was most likely calling for more capital. By this time John Shakespeare had established himself as a Stratford wool-stapler, and was evidently building up a respectable business and making a steady advance in wealth and civic importance. His avocation covered a variety of occupations, such as glover, gauntlet-maker, leather-curer and bootmaker, cattle and corn merchant, grazier, butcher, and fellmonger. The wool-staple was one of the most important industries in Warwickshire, and Stratford and Warwick were well-known centres; the ancient arms of the borough contained those of the Merchants of the Staple, and the popular estimation of the trade may be judged from the writer of the *Golden Fleece*, who, in 1657, terms it " the flower and strength, the revenue and bloud of England, the milk and honey of the grasier and countryman, in a word, the very exchequer of wealth." This business, with its many modes of activity, would account for the glove-making and calf-killing legends with which we are all so familiar, and also explains the rapid advance of this worthy Merchant of the Staple. The year 1557 marks also his first step upon the civic ladder, in his appointment to the supervision of breweries and bakeries within the borough; and during the next twelve years he filled intervening posts, until he reached the highest honour in 1569, and became High Bailiff of the Borough.

Early in 1557, the Government of Philip and Mary, carrying out a policy which had for its object the complete ascendency of the old Faith in the public as well as the private lives of the citizens of England, granted a commission to Bonner wherein the widest powers of coercion and persecution were committed to his discretion. Courts of Inquisition were established in every borough, and all justices of the peace and men in authority were compelled to take oath on the matter of their own faithfulness, and swear to aid the commissioners in the prosecution of those who refused to attend church or abstained from worship according to the rites of the Roman Catholic faith. The Englishman's instinctive hatred of intolerant persecution had made many men in office shield their reforming brethren and caused others to refuse to accept positions under Bonner's persecuting commissions. It was obvious that the policy could not be carried out successfully unless determined Roman Catholics were in positions of authority, hence Bonner sent down injunctions to the effect that steadfast men were to be placed in office, and that attendance at the borough meetings was to be strictly enforced. Reluctant councillors were compelled by enactment to accept office and discharge the duties thereof faithfully. We have the traces of this movement in the borough enactments of September 29th, 1557, when the following rules were framed to compel the attendance of reluctant councillors :—

" Stratford Records, 29*th Sept.* 1557.

" A fine of xxs. is to be imposed upon Aldermen and xs. for capytall burgesez who do not attend the yearly election of Bailiff.

Earlier Years of John Shakespeare

" Fine for refusal of the office of Bailiff, xli. (£10).[1]

" Fine for refusal of the office of Chief Alderman vIIjli. (£8).

" Item, that ther be ones every monethe yn the yere at least a hall to be kept in the Councell Chambur, and that every Alderman and capytall burgese be then and ther present under the peyn to forfeit every offender vjs. viijd. and that to be payd at or before the next hall then and ther holden to the use of the Chamber except a lawfull cawse or lycence unto hym or them given by the Belyf.

" Item, that every Alderman and capytall burgese be personally at every hall upon warning to them geven or els to shewe a lawfull cawse why they cannot be ther, unto the Baylyffe before the Halle be gathered and to agree unto all such orders as shalbe ther made in his absence, in payne of forfettynge for every default xIjd."

It will be clearly seen that enactments such as these go much deeper than mere resolutions of Council for the purpose of ensuring a fair attendance. Men were wilfully holding back from office, and it had become necessary for authority to be applied with severity.

During this year one Robert Perrot was Bailiff of Stratford, and it may be taken for granted that before so important an office was offered to

---

[1] " The relative value of money in Shakspere's time and ours may be roughly computed at one-twelfth in articles of trade, and one-twentieth in landed or house property."— HALLIWELL PHILLIPPS.

and accepted by him in times of bitter persecution under a most bigoted King and Queen, it was well known that he was sound in the faith and an ardent and pronounced Roman Catholic. It was intended that he should take part, as chief magistrate of a borough, in Bonner's policy of enforcing conformity, and therefore it would be necessary for him to be of the ancient Faith.

But the country was nearer release than anyone anticipated; the death of Mary in November 1558 brought her Protestant sister Elizabeth to the throne, and immediately there was a return of exiles and a popular rising against Roman Catholicism. People and Queen alike had cause to resent Papal supremacy, and for a time full vent was given to revengeful feelings.

Elizabeth could not forgive the insulting words of Pope Paul IV., who contemptuously said on the news of her accession, "that she could not succeed, being a bastard, and that the Crown of England being a fief of the Popedom, she had been guilty of great presumption in assuming it without his consent." And her people could not forget the fires of Smithfield.

The Queen entered upon her policy of defiance

with all the Tudor spirit ; and the Acts of Supremacy and Uniformity of Worship were one answer to the Pope, and the Commission to destroy all Altars, Crosses, and Vaine Symbols another. Zeal soon outruns discretion in a crusade of destruction, and bigoted Protestants began to lay themselves open to charges as severe as those urged against Bonner's inquisitors during the late reign. The Queen found it necessary to forbid any further demolition of images and symbols. The county of Warwickshire was one of the first to become conspicuous for its adherence to the tenets of the more thoroughgoing among the Reformers. Puritan ministers were so plentiful in Coventry that at one time the Mayor levied a tax upon every householder for their maintenance. In 1560 Mass was put down in the town amid scenes of great enthusiasm, and images and popish relics were burnt in the public streets. The Puritan party in the county was of a most influential character. The Earl of Leicester, the Earl of Warwick, Job Throgmorton of Haseley, Robert Wigston of Woolston, John Hales of Coventry, were prominent laymen ; Humphrey Fenn for forty years preached the

22 *Shakespeare : Puritan and Recusant*

gospel in Coventry; Thomas Lever was archdeacon in the same town; Edward Lord and Hugh Clark were vicars of Woolston, John Hooke and Ephraim Hewet vicars of Wroxhall, Samuel Clark of Alcester, John Oxenbridge of Coventry, Richard Byfield of Stratford, and Thomas Cartwright (leader of the movement) of Warwick. Some of the most eminent leaders of the Puritans were ministers of Warwickshire. It must be remembered that with the exception of some strong Gospellers, descendants of Wycliffe's preaching brothers, and professing generally the principles of what is now known as the Baptist Church, there were no Dissenters in England at this time. Despite the persecutions and confusion all parties were gathered within the one National Church. Papist, Prelatist, and Puritan were each fighting for the supremacy, and each hoped to force the others to adopt his views. It was not until the year of the Papal Excommunication of Elizabeth in 1570 that the Roman Catholic broke away entirely from the Established Church. Repressive and intolerant measures were destroying the hopes raised in Mary's reign, but English Romanists clung most devotedly to the Church until persecution and the Papal Excommunication rendered any further tolerance impossible.

On the other side, the Prelatist, or Queen's Churchman, was gradually gaining power, for the Queen's actions showed that all her thoughts lay in the direction of assuming ecclesiastical supremacy in the realm of England. She showed her hand cautiously, for the Puritan bulwark was too strong to be thrown aside suddenly; but as years went on it was clearly seen that the growth of Puritanism was distasteful to her, and the repressive measures adopted proved that she was prepared to go almost any length in her efforts to crush it out. But in the first years of her reign English refugees from the Presbyterian Churches of the Continent had been brought over to officiate in high ecclesiastical duties, and the English people looked naturally to the various Reformed Churches of Europe for example and guidance. Popular feeling was against High Church doctrines and anything that savoured of Rome; the Universities were Puritan to the core; and even those men who afterwards became notorious for their Prelacy, like Whitgift of Canterbury, Sandys of Worcester, and Aylmer of London, "that gote heard prowde," were Puritan enough to protest against the "unlawfulness of the habits," and to declaim against "the relics of the Amorites." Elizabeth knew her own mind on the subject of religion, and revealed it as policy dictated. She needed a strong defence against the vigorous Roman Catholicism of the North of England, as well as against the aggressive and murderous fanaticism of Spain and France, and she found this in the sturdy hater of Rome, the Puritan. Papal intrigues both at home and abroad forced her to keep an ever-watchful eye upon her enemies; and deeming it not politic to alienate a powerful section of her subjects, she gave hopes of a reformation of the Church on thorough lines. She thus won the Puritan almost entirely over to her side, and among her subjects she could reckon no more earnest and enthusiastic supporter.

In the year 1559, the first year of Elizabeth, and a strongly Protestant one, Adrian Quyney became Bailiff of Stratford, and his lifelong friend John Shakespeare also accepted office in the Court Leet,

Earlier Years of John Shakespeare   25

and became one of the adjudicators of fines for offences treated summarily.

In 1563 John Tayler and John Shakespeare submit the borough accounts as chamberlains. In the autumn of the same year John Shakespeare is fined for a breach of borough sanitary byelaws, and on 20th December he is first mentioned as a "capytall burgese" in a deed relating to a "tenneimente in the Rother Street."

The annual accounts as submitted by the chamberlains are full of interest because John Shakespeare is mentioned for *four successive years*, and in connection with business which throws a revealing sidelight upon the question of his religious sympathies.

The chamberlains were appointed for the purpose of transacting Council business and keeping the various accounts of the year; they submitted their abstracts year by year, signed and sealed for the sanction of the Council.

On 10th January 1564 the accounts are presented in the names of John Tayler and John Shakespeare, and an indication of strong Protestant feeling is given in the attention directed to the refitting of the old Chapel, a place of worship which was directly under the supervision of the Town Council. It was a case of alteration rather than of renovation. Timber was purchased for the seating of the place, Roman Catholic emblems were torn down or defaced, and from the state of the mutilations as recorded by Dugdale it is clear that these alterations were carried out in a thoroughly Puritan spirit.

"The most ancient pictures," writes Dugdale (p. 103), "were in the chancel, and many parts of them, particularly the crosses, had been evidently mutilated with a sharp instrument by the ill-directed zeal of our early reformers." "The lower compartment was one of those intentionally mutilated, a cross, an altar, and a crucifix."

Further significance is given to the proceedings in that they took place two years after the proclamation which the Queen issued (2nd Eliz.) against a recurrence of the outbreak which occurred on her accession, and this shows that a more vigorous Puritan element was working in the Council, wherein Adrian Quiney, Richard Hill, John Wheler, John Tayler, and John Shakespeare were prominent members; and from the fact that John Shakespeare supplied the timber, claimed a fee, had a standing account, and submitted the yearly accounts on four occasions, it seems more than probable that the alterations were carried out under his active supervision. It is not necessary to point out that the demolition of a Roman Catholic place of worship would not have been undertaken by Roman Catholics, for this would naturally be most abhorrent work to them, and the man would be a disgrace to the old Faith who took an active and leading part in it.

The accounts as submitted contained the following:—

"*Jan.* 10*th*, 1564.

"Item, peyd to Shakspeyr for a pece tymbur IIJs.

"Item, payd for defasyng ymages in the Chapell IJs.

"Item, Chamburlens fee XXs.

"Sicut remaynythe Vs. IXd. which is delyvered into the handes of William Tyler and William Smythe, newe Chamburlens so that they befor named John Taylor and John Shakysper have made a true and lawful accompt for ther tyme beyng Chamburlens

"Et sic quieti sunt Johannes Taylor et Johannes Shakspeyr.

"*Jan.* 24*th*, 1564.

"Item, at this Hall the Chamber ys found in arrerage and ys in det unto John Shakysper XXVs. VIIJd.'

Two new chamberlains had been appointed for the year 1564, but in submitting the accounts for March 21st, 1565, they evidently defer to the experience of John Shakysper and John Taylor and allow them to make out the accounts.

"*March 21st*, 1565. The accompt of William Tyler and William Smythe, Chamburlens, made by John Shakysper and John Tayler, for one whol yere endyng at the Feest of Sent Mychell Archaungell now past.

" Item, payd for taking doune rood loft in the Chapell IJs."

In the next year John Shakespeare again made out the accounts, and this time his name stands alone.

"*Feb. 13th*, 1566.

"The accompt of William Tylor and William Smythe, made by John Shaksper the xvth day of February, in the eighth yere of the reigne of our sovereign Lady Elizabeth by the Grace of God of Englond, Fraunce, and Irelonde, Quene, Defender of the feith etc. for one yere ending at the Feest of Sent Mychell thararchangell now last past, ut sequitur."

The list of payments which follows is chiefly for repairs at the Chapel and Schoolhouse, showing that the work was still proceeding under the direction of John Shakespeare. An item which occurs in this account is worth noting, inasmuch as it shows light on several controverted points. The words are—

"Item, payd to Shakspeyr for a rest of old det £3, 2s. 7d."

It has been readily accepted by many that John Shakespeare was an illiterate man, and that the fact of a writ being issued against a tradesman is enough to stamp him as poverty-stricken. Let us take the latter point first. In 1586, under date January 19th, a writ was issued against John Shakespeare, and it was returned to the Court with the words written upon it "quod praedictus Johannes Shackspere nihil habet unde distringere potest." This writ has been considered a strong link in a chain of evidence by which John Shakespeare is supposed in 1586 to have been meshed in inextricable financial difficulties, plunged into a poverty so complete that it has ended his civic life, caused his eldest son to be removed prematurely from a *free* school in order to eke out a livelihood for a bankrupt father and mother, and cast so deep a shadow upon the erstwhile successful merchant's life that he has to skulk in byways to avoid arrest, and even to forsake the public worship of

God. And yet it is incontestable that at the time the "nihil habet unde distringere potest" was written he was holding valuable property in Stratford and the neighbourhood, was witnessing wills and fulfilling positions of trust, and had not a single action for debt against him.

We cannot at this day explain the meaning of the words, or how far the writ had power, but it is undeniable that so far as landed property was concerned John Shakespeare had plenty to distrain upon.

Mr. Halliwell Phillipps says, regarding the writ of 1586: "The reader must be warned from these, which might appear in the brief record as conveying inferences against the prosperity of John Shakespeare's circumstances, but which do not when thus exhibited in particulars, that he cannot use these entries in every case as a history of his pecuniary affairs. The ancient forms of process in actions for debt must also be considered, and it will, I think, be found that even the most formidable circumstance which is entered under the date of January 19th, 1586, 'quod praedictus Johannes Shackspere nihil habet unde distringere potest' must be construed in great measure by legal formality, not necessarily as an actual fact."

And if the words "nihil habet" must be construed in great measure by legal formality, the fact of having a writ served upon him would not in any way support the poverty theory of John Shakespeare's life; and here we return to our argument derived from the annual accounts of the chamberlains twenty years before this date, that is in 1566. In that year Mr. Alderman Shakespeare's financial position was a most stable one, for besides the pecuniary legacy and the reversions under Robert Arden's will, and his own property in and about Stratford, his business was prospering so well that he could afford to have a running account with the borough without troubling much about "arrerages." As a matter of fact the town owed him a fair sum. His civic position had been attested by his election to the position of Alderman in July 1565, yet in September 1566 a precept to the Sergeants at Mace was issued to distrain on his goods and chattels to answer the suit of one Joan Pagge.

"Preceptum est servientibus ad clavam quod distringatis, seu unum vestrum distringat Johannem Shakespere per omnia bona et cattalla sua, ita quod sit apud proximam curiam de recordo tentam ibidem ad respondendum Johanne Pagge de placito debiti etc.

"Datum sub sigillo mea xj mo die Septembris anno regni domine Elizabethe Dei gracia Anglie etc. Octavo.

"HENRICUS HYGFORD, Senescallus."

It is obvious from Alderman Shakespeare's *known* possessions at this time that it would be ridiculous to accept this writ as an evidence of his poverty. Writs are not uncommon with business men of a litigious nature, and John Shakespeare was a man who usually fought a question to the bitter end, as witness his actions to recover the estate of Asbies from his kinsman Lambart, his stubborn fight against Nicholas Lane, and his threescore and ten recorded lawsuits.

Rightly considered, the writ of 1586 with its "nihil habet" ought to be taken as an evidence of times of dangerous persecution and accompanying necessary safeguarding, instead of a proof of poverty, for religious intolerance and ecclesiastical

[1] See Appendix *B*.

Earlier Years of John Shakespeare 33

espionage had made suspected men cautious; and the Puritan spirit which conceived and carried out the demolition of Roman Catholic symbols and the sale of Papist vestments would be apt to find itself endangered by the terribly severe laws passed by Elizabeth to enforce Protestant conformity.

Again returning to the line which appears in the accounts, "payd to Shakspeyr for a rest of old det," let us consider the question of the alleged illiterateness of the Shakespeares.

Most biographers agree with Halliwell Phillipps when he writes (p. 38): "Although both his parents were absolutely illiterate, they had the sagacity to appreciate the importance of an education for their son, and the poet somehow or other was taught to read and write, the necessary preliminaries to admission into the free school."

"Fortunately for us, the youthful dramatist had, excepting in the schoolroom, little opportunity of studying anything but a grander volume, the Infinite book of Nature."

"Removed prematurely from school, residing in a bookless neighbourhood, thrown into the midst of occupations adverse to scholastic progress, it is difficult to believe that when he first left Stratford, he was not all but destitute of polished accomplishments."

These are sweeping deductions when we consider that the sole ground upon which they are made is the fact that John Shakespeare and his wife attested documents by a mark instead of a signature, a common enough practice in earlier and later days which by no means implies absolute illiterateness.

It is absurd to single out Stratford as a bookless and illiterate neighbourhood; it was neither more nor less than any other country town within easy reach of Oxford; it had its scholars, its preachers, and its schoolmasters; honest burghers, kinsmen of Shakespeare, could write Latin as an ordinary means of correspondence, and there are many evidences which go to show that Stratford took a keen and intelligent interest in the religious, political, and literary movements of the day.

So far as the father of William Shakespeare was concerned, he was looked upon by those who knew him best as a prosperous and able man, a skilful accountant, a capable speaker, and one who could be trusted to represent the interests of the town in the Parliamentary Councils at London; an honoured chief magistrate and bailiff; his numerous lawsuits show that his business transactions covered a wide area, and the legal knowledge required for many of the functions he performed could not have been gained entirely by experience. Here, in the case of the chamberlain's accounts before us, he is either the supervisor of the Puritan alterations in the Chapel, or his skill as a public accountant is being acknowledged; and if one were trying to emulate the victories of textual criticism, an argument might be adduced to show that he himself was the writer of these accounts from the fact that the words "paid to *Shakspeyr* for a rest of old det" occur. Aldermen were always designated in writing by the prefix "Mr."; unobservant people may assert that newly-fledged aldermen are not usually insistent upon the due recognition of their new dignity, yet clerks and scriveners would be mindful of it, especially to one employing them. If Tylor and Smythe, the chamberlains, were good penmen but poor accountants, trusting to clearer heads for guidance through figures, they would naturally, and as a matter of ordinary courtesy, have written the customary "Mr." before Alderman Shakespeare's name. It was his official designation, and would certainly have been inserted by them, and, indeed, by any man who had cause to write it, *except the alderman himself*.

Again, was the wife of John Shakespeare, the gentle Mary Arden, bookless and absolutely illiterate, and did she turn her eldest son out into the world "destitute of polished accomplishments," and having had but "little opportunity of studying anything"? or is this only another gratuitous assumption? The phrase "destitute of polished accomplishments" is capable of many interpretations, but it is certain that in twelve years, from the time he quitted Stratford, William Shakespeare did what few men before or since have ever succeeded in doing, he made a fortune, wrote marvellous books, and educated himself at the same time. Most men find that the struggle with the world leaves little time for polished accomplishment unless the education is there to begin with. If a man makes money he usually finds its possession his sole accomplishment. But William

Shakespeare, it may be objected, was the possessor of unequalled genius, and therefore achievements were possible to him which were impossible to the ordinary man.

That is true, but there is at least one thing which the most brilliant intellect cannot give a man, and which even the mighty Shakespeare would have lacked if he had had to obtain it after he began writing. *We mean the power of accurate and literal quotation,* in the poet's case not exhibited in classical learning, but in *an extensive and wonderfully accurate knowledge of the actual words of Holy Scripture.*[1]

The most cursory study of his works reveals his power of biblical quotation; and it is clear that his mind must have been literally steeped in scriptural thought and language, for Bible thoughts in Bible words are worked into the very warp and woof of his plays. Now, a man may learn much in later life and be able to quote with some degree of freedom, but he never attains the power evidenced by Shakespeare, unless he has from his earliest days been trained in Bible study.

[1] See Appendix *A*.

38 *Shakespeare : Puritan and Recusant*

Before words and phrases rise instinctively to the thought and pen as vehicles of expression, they must have been lodged in the mind in the earliest days of youth; and it is no exaggeration to say that if William Shakespeare had spent the whole of his first twelve years in London in exclusive study of the Word of God, it is questionable if even then he could have attained the perfect ease of quotation he manifests.

There is only one time in life when this power may be won, and the best place to learn it is at that point and focus of all scriptural attainments, the mother's knee and in the home circle, when, as a little child, the words of the Bible are dropped into the heart and memory.

If Mary Shakespeare could not read and write her own name, she could at least teach her son the "polished accomplishment" of insight into the words of the Revelation of God.

And this raises a wider and more important question still as to the character of the home wherein daily Bible instruction in the vulgar tongue must have been made the rule of the household.

Was it a Roman Catholic home? Was this

Earlier Years of John Shakespeare

feature then, or is it now, a prominent characteristic of Roman Catholic teaching? If Shakespeare learned his Scripture from the Vulgate, how comes it that he does not quote it with his own words of translation and refrain from using the very words of the English Bible? The Douai Bible was not published until 1609, when Shakespeare was a man of over fifty years of age, with most of his work done, so this version is out of the question. Had the poet the gift of prophecy as well as of genius, that he could quote in the common speech the very words of English translators from his reading of a Romish Bible?

Again, is it not an established fact that throughout the whole of these religious controversies the bitterest animosity was shown to the Bible by the Papal authorities and Romish priesthood and laity? The Bible typified to the Papist the Puritan religion, just as images and crosses typified Roman Catholicism to the Puritan. Wherever a popular rising occurred, the Protestant broke the images and tore down the crosses, and the Papist burned the Bibles. The Roman Catholic insurgents in Durham Cathedral showed their hatred to

Protestantism by slashing the hateful books with their daggers and burning all the Bibles they could lay hands upon in the sacred precincts. Domestic piety of a high character was certainly known and cherished in the homes of earnest and godly Roman Catholics, but it was a piety fostered by books other than the Bible in the English tongue, and founded upon priestly instruction and missals and books of devotions. From 1560 there was only *one* great Bible of the households of England, and that, as we shall show later, was the Puritan Bible of Geneva, and more than once in the years of Elizabeth even this book was unpossessed (because of prohibitions) save by the households of earnest Puritans. Nor must we overlook the fact that the Bible in the vulgar tongue has always been a strictly prohibited book to the Roman Catholic. Despite denials and explanations, the fourth rule of the Council of Trent seems to be explicit enough on this point.

"Whereas it is manifest by experience that if the Holy Bible translated into the vulgar tongue be allowed indifferently to anybody, then on account of men's rashness will arise from hence a greater detriment than advantage.

"If any one without a licence presume to read or keep by him the Bible he shall be disqualified to receive the absolution of his sins till he deliver it up to the ordinary" (Regulae Indices S.S. Synodi Tridentinae jussu editae. De lib. prohib. reg. 4).

Pope Clement VIII., commenting upon the rule of Pius IV., adds in reference to the sentence "without a licence" explanatory words full of significance.

"This law is not to be understood as if by it the Bishops, Inquisitors, or heads of Convents were invested with power to grant licences, read, buy, or keep the Bible translated into the vulgar language, seeing hitherto by the order and practice of the Holy Roman and Universal Inquisition the power had been taken away from them to grant licences to read or keep the whole Bible in the vulgar tongue, or any other part of the Holy Scriptures of the Old or New Testaments published in any vulgar language, all which is to be inviolably observed" (Index lib. Prohib. S.D.N.

Clementus P.P. VIII. jussu recognitus et publicatus).

We need not trouble about Protestant witnesses on this matter, for Rome herself has always been outspoken, and is the best testimony as to the way in which this antagonism to the spread of a vernacular Bible among her people has been fostered and commended; she is frankly and continually antagonistic, as may be seen by little study.

Cardinal Bellarmine, the great Papist authority, says:

"We maintain that the Scriptures ought not to be read publicly in the vulgar tongue, nor allowed to be read indifferently by everybody."

In the present century Pope Pius VII., in 1816, in a Bull issued against Bible Societies, said:

"Agreeably to the Index, the Bible printed by heretics is to be numbered among other prohibited books, for it is evident from experience that the Holy Scriptures when circulated in the vulgar tongue have, through the temerity of men, produced more harm than benefit." He then goes on to describe the operations of the Bible Societies as

Earlier Years of John Shakespeare 43

" pestilential and defiling, a crafty device by which the very foundations of religion are undermined. A pestilence which must be remedied and abolished, a defilement of the faith, eminently dangerous to souls, impious machinations of innovators, wickedness of a nefarious scheme, snares prepared for men's souls, everlasting ruin. A new species of tares which an adversary has abundantly sown."

Cardinal Wiseman has followed in the same line in his book the *Catholic Doctrine of the Bible*; he does not pretend for one moment to obscure the issue, and not only avows the shutting up of God's Word to the people, but glories in avowing it, and rejoices in the policy.

" If therefore we be asked," he says (p. 20), " why we do not give the Bible indifferently to all, and the shutting up of God's Word be disdainfully thrown in our face, we will not seek to elude the question, or meet the taunts by denial or by attempts to prove that our principles on the subject are not antagonistic to those of Protestants. They are antagonistic, and we glory in avowing it."

In the Roman Catholic newspaper the *Tablet*, under date December 17th, 1853, a priest is reported to have said that, "he would rather a Catholic should read the worst works of immorality than the Protestant Bible, that forgery of God's Word, that slander of Christ."

It is no straining of argument to use these opinions of pope, cardinal, and priest, as indicating the strong feeling which has always existed in the Roman Catholic Church against a free study of the Bible in the vernacular; and if it is true to-day, when religious liberty is assured, and Bibles may be obtained by everyone, what must it have been in the days of Elizabeth, a day's march from the Reformation, when Protestant and Papist were hounding each other to the death? It would be an astonishing thing, and one absolutely unique, to find a Roman Catholic training his child in the very book that his fellow-religionists hated and his Church proscribed. Even if a Papist obtained a Bible out of curiosity, much as a Puritan might become possessed of a Manual of Devotions, it is inconceivable that he would immediately adopt the proscribed book as a basis for his own household training, and personally instruct his children in its words, in defiance of his own religious sentiments

Earlier Years of John Shakespeare 45

and the unchanging and most bitter denunciations of his Church. It is a poor theory which is forced to make John Shakespeare an utter scoundrel before it can present him as a fellow-religionist; indeed, the Roman Catholic who despoils chapels of their religious symbols, tears down crosses and mutilates sacred images in the discharge of public duty, and trains his household in Puritan methods with a Protestant Bible, is one whom the present day might possibly understand and tolerate, but who would be incomprehensible to that sterner age which produced the religious bitternesses of the days of Elizabeth and the earlier Stuarts. It is hard to believe that the Bible knowledge of William Shakespeare and the iconoclastic tendencies of his father were derived from the Roman Catholic Church. This is a long digression from the chamberlain accounts of 1563-66, but the questions arise naturally from the subject. We return to the events of 1564 as recorded in Stratford history. On April 26th of this year, "Gulielmus, filius Johannes Shakspere" was baptized in the Church of the Holy Trinity, Stratford.

During the year the plague visited the town, and

carried off many of its leading inhabitants; subscriptions were raised for the relief of the poor. A very interesting peep into the informal nature of some of the Council meetings is given in the record of August 30th, 1564, where a pleasing picture is conjured up of the fathers of the borough meeting under the pleasant shades of the trees, while the sunlit Avon flowed gently before them. They had met for a good purpose.

"At a Hall holdyn in oure garden the 30th daye of Auguste, A° 1564, moneye payd towardes the releff of the povre."

Mr. Balye leads off with a subscription of 3s. 6d. Mr. Alderman John Wheler gives 2s. 6d.; the burgesses follow suit with subscriptions of varying amounts, John Shakespeare giving 12d., and the poorest or thriftiest putting himself down for 4d.

Then on September 6th another collection is made, being "money gathered towards the releff of those that be vysyted."

Mr. Quyney gives 17d., John Shakespeare 6d., and Richard Hylle (a well-to-do man) 2d. The heavy visitation does not seem to have decreased much, and a few days later, September 27th (at what

Earlier Years of John Shakespeare

were evidently emergency Council meetings), another subscription was taken " towards the povre of oure town." Mr. Balye gives 12d., John Shakespeare 6d., and Richard Hylle, who on this occasion evidently remembered his purse, contributed 12d.

At the Council meeting in September it was usual for the borough to elect the officers to serve during the ensuing year, and on the 27th September Mr. John Wheler was elected bailiff, but managed to postpone his service for another year, and Richard Hylle was chosen in his place.

On October 20th Mr. Hylle contributes to the poor fund 16 pence, Alderman John Wheler 12 pence, while Burgess John Shakespeare gives 8 pence.

A few months pass by and John Shakespeare rises a step on the civic ladder, and is appointed an alderman of the borough. On September 12th it is recorded that he took the necessary oaths of allegiance to Queen Elizabeth.

"*July 4th*, 1565. At thys halle John Shakspeyr is appointed an Alderman."

"*Sept.* 12th. Johne Shakspeyr jur. on this day" (*i.e.* took the oaths).

October 4th brings the nomination of a new bailiff

48 *Shakespeare: Puritan and Recusant*

to the front once more, and Mr. Alderman John Wheler, who had been offered the position the previous year, was again nominated, and this time accepts the office. Mr. Wheler was an intimate and lifelong friend of John Shakespeare, and throughout the whole of his life in Stratford was closely associated with him. Early in the Council the names of the two men are bracketed together, and the connection thus formed continues through the Town Council records. We find them associated together at Council meetings, upon public committees, in civic and national causes; and after taking part in many of the most pronounced Puritan movements of the town, are together dismissed the Council on the same day, and a few years later are returned as Recusants in the well-known Recusancy Return of Sir Thomas Lucy in 1592.

II

"Queen, Prelatist, and Puritan against Roman Catholic"

CHAPTER II

"QUEEN, PRELATIST, AND PURITAN AGAINST ROMAN CATHOLIC"

THE year 1567 saw Elizabeth dealing skilfully with the difficult questions which made the early period of her government a ceaseless anxiety. Religious antipathy was being still further accentuated by reason of the never-ending Papal intrigues, and the unfortunate Roman Catholics were subjected to an antagonism which was bitter, cruel, and constant. The Queen, dominating her Council, was launching schemes intended for the enforcement of absolute conformity within the Established Church; it was commanded that exact order and uniformity was to be maintained in all external rites and ceremonies, none were to be admitted to ecclesiastical preferment unless they had first of all promised to comply with the demands of the law, and the laity were ordered on pain of severe penalty to keep in faithful attendance at their parish churches. A case of opposition soon arose in London, where some thirty persons were arrested in Plumbers' Hall, Anchor Lane, and charged with contravening the ecclesiastical laws and using a Service Book other than that of the Common Prayer. They had set up a separate conventicle, and expected sympathy from the Reformers on the Continent, but it is noteworthy that Knox, Beza, Bullinger, and others deprecated any separation from the National Church. Neal sums it up aptly when he says: "Most of the Puritans were unwilling to separate from a Church where the Word and Sacraments were truly administered, though defiled with some popish superstitions." But although Elizabeth was inclined to deal harshly with her own nonconforming subjects, she extended a hearty welcome to those sufferers for religion who had been driven out of the Netherlands and France by the cruelties of Alva, and the victories of the Henri's of Guise and Anjou; she granted full privileges of worship to them, but at the same time intimated that they would forfeit these if they received into their Presbyterian communion any of her subjects of England.

Their coming to England made a deep impression upon the people, and gave emphasis to the dread of Romish ascendency. The public mind was at this time greatly excited. Mary of Scotland had been deposed and detained a virtual prisoner in England; assassins were known to be on the track of William the Silent and Coligny; and disturbing rumours of Papal deposition and excommunication of Elizabeth had more than once disturbed England.

The first move was made in the North by the Earls of Westmorland and Northumberland, who gathered the Roman Catholic gentry together in a plot which had for its object the uniting of all Papists in proclaiming Mary of Scots Queen of England.

The insurrection rapidly assumed threatening proportions, but Elizabeth met the danger with her accustomed coolness and promptitude. In the first place, levies were drawn principally from

Warwickshire and Worcestershire for service in the North (see county records), and the Puritan Earl of Warwick was placed in command. Opportunity was then taken to test the faithfulness of men in official positions, and a profession of allegiance to Elizabeth was required from all justices of the peace and officers in commission throughout all the counties of England; they were ordered to subscribe their names to an instrument professing their conformity and obedience to the Act of Uniformity.

On November 10th, a certain Dr. Norton, who had been a prebendary of York in Queen Mary's time, came from Rome with the title of Apostolic Penitentiary, and went about the northern counties inciting the Roman Catholics to rebellion by stating that the Pope was about to issue a bull of excommunication against Elizabeth.

On November 14th the insurgents marched to Durham Cathedral and took possession of it. They hunted out all the English Bibles and Prayer Books, and slashed them in pieces with their daggers, and then in a fervour of devotion knelt while Mass was said for the last time

"Queen, Prelatist, and Puritan"

in any of the old cathedrals of England. A few days later, the Earl of Warwick came up with his levies, and the rising was dispersed without the striking of a blow. Measures were at once adopted to safeguard the cause of this disturbance; Mary of Scotland was removed from Tutbury in Staffordshire to the safer keeping of the Puritan stronghold of Coventry, and all access to her was strictly prohibited.

Warwickshire as a county had evidenced intense loyalty in this juncture. Was Stratford slumbering while all these alarms and excursions were proceeding, and when Mary, the Roman Catholic hope, was a prisoner a few miles away?

It is significant that in the midst of these disturbances in 1568, John Shakespeare was nominated and made Bailiff of the Borough. Almost the first enactment of his year was one directed against those citizens and office-bearers who were beginning to feel the severity of the restrictions against the old Faith.

It will be remembered that in the persecuting year of Bonner's commission, Robert Perrot had been made Bailiff of Stratford, and that measures were then taken to enforce Roman Catholicism with the acceptance of office.

On October 1st, 1568, the Stratford Council, under the active superintendence of John Shakespeare as bailiff, and John Wheler and Adrian Quyney as aldermen, passed the following enactment concerning the fines to be levied upon recalcitrant aldermen and burgesses:—

"Anyone refusing shall forfect to the use of the Bayliffe and Burgesses £3, 6s. 8d., and if the same person or persons that soe doe forfecte the sayd sum doe nat pay the same to the Chamberleynes of the said Burrowe for the time being within three days after demande made, that then he or they that so do shall make defaulte to forfecte to the use of the sayd Chamber the some of fortye shyllings in nomine pene to be forfeited and payd from hall to hall untyll the same person or persons callyd as ys afforesaid doe yelde hymself to be a burges, and the lyke forfecture and peyne shall be levied upon Aldermen for neglect."

This enactment is much more severe than that of Perrot's in that the penalty is made a concurrent one "to be payd from hall to hall," the object plainly being to compel attendance by heavy monthly fines. It was aimed chiefly at what may be termed passive resistance on the part of Roman Catholics, for active hostility to Elizabeth would have been terminated in a quicker fashion than warnings and fines.

Was it the irony of fate that the ex-Bailiff of Stratford who had held office in the last year of the persecuting Mary should be the first to feel the sting of an enactment which was directed exclusively against the Roman Catholics? for it was Mr. Robert Perrot who was the first man to fall beneath the Puritan enthusiasm of the Council of which John Shakespeare was chief magistrate. And it is significant of John Shakespeare's energy that this prosecution was carried through with rather more earnestness than one would expect from one neighbour towards another.

Mr. Robert Perrot had made himself conspicuous by his absence from Council meetings in the stirring days which led up to the Northern disturbances, and in the months of 1569, when the persecution of Roman Catholics had received such an impetus.

The Stratford Records tell us how John Shakespeare dealt with him.

"*Sept. 7th*, 1569.

"Before Mr. John Shakysper, Hyzgh Balyf and Mr. John Wheler, Alderman.

"Mr. Perrot for his wilfull absentyng of hymself, hys fine is £5."

And then follows this most important statement :—

"Mr Perrot hathe byn dyvers tymes requyred and by the said Mr. Balyfe's commandment warned to make his apparaunce at the hall and Councell howse for the sayd burrowe to accompanye the sayd Balyf and others burgesses to consyder of such matters as in that place we have usyd to doe, chefely for the servyce unto the Quenes Maieste, when wee be requyred to the same, the said Mr. Perrot nothing regarding his duty to our sayd Quene, wylfully, frowardly, and obstynately refusyth to repayre to the sayd Chamber."

Here the charge against Perrot is one of passive opposition and withdrawal; when severe measures are being enforced against Roman Catholics, he was forgetting "his duty to our sayd Quene."

Such a charge could not possibly have been made against a Queen's Churchman, for the essence of his creed was unquestioning loyalty to the Queen in matters spiritual and temporal; nor could it have been made against a Puritan,

"Queen, Prelatist, and Puritan" 59

for Elizabeth had not yet entered upon her course of repression and persecution, and the Puritan, always loyal, was heart and soul with Elizabeth against popish intrigues, and looked for much from her as a reward of faithfulness. It could only apply to the Roman Catholics, against whom severe enactments were being put into force, and who, at this time, were thoroughly distrusted, and hated as traitors and would-be assassins by the majority of Englishmen. Bailiff John Shakespeare and Alderman John Wheler acted with stern promptitude in dealing with their old colleague and fellow-townsman.

The meeting of the 7th September was adjourned from the Wednesday to the Friday in order to give Mr. Perrot an opportunity of putting in his attendance, and to make sure the sergeants were ordered to arrest him and bring him to the meeting. If Mr. Perrot managed to elude the vigilance of the sergeants, and still persisted in his obstinacy, the penalty was declared against him.

"Upon peyne to forfect to the use of the Chamber, if he make default, twentye pounds, and fyve pounds at everye hall hereafter to be holden within the said Burrow until he doe yelde hymself, and also if any of the bretherne of the sayd corporation and their successors shall wylfully refuse to come to their assemblies, that they shall forfeit to the Chamber for everye defaulte fyve pounds, onless he be sycke or in the Quenes Majesty's service."

On Friday, 9th September, the fateful day for Mr. Perrot, it is recorded in the Stratford Records:

"Before Mr. Shakysper, hyzgh Balyf.
"At thys Hall the sayd Mr. Robert Perrot wylfully made default and forfected the sayd peyne of xx £."

We need not dwell upon the heaviness of this fine, nor upon the fact of the recurrent penalty for non-attendance, for it is evident that a prosecution carried forward with such fervour would not be likely to err on the side of mercy. A more interesting portion of the enactment is given in the words "if any of the bretherne of the sayd corporation and their successors shall wylfully refuse to come to their assemblies, that they shall forfect to the Chamber for everye defaulte fyve pounds, onless he be sycke or in the Quenes Majesty's service," for this is levelled at more than the individual case of Robert Perrot. It was a menace at all peace-loving

"Queen, Prelatist, and Puritan" 61

Roman Catholics who favoured passive opposition and refused to set the machinery of persecution against members of their own Faith, but it was also a weapon which was used against the Protestant when the Puritan was being harried, and both John Shakespeare and John Wheler felt the pain of it when in later years they wilfully and obstinately refused to attend Council meetings where measures to compel Puritan conformity were under discussion; and when because they would not join in this persecution they were compelled to risk and meet heavy recurrent fines, and in the end be dismissed the Council.

But the Puritan of 1569 could hardly have realised that in 1590 Elizabeth would proceed to extremities in her insistence upon conformity in worship.

Seven months after Robert Perrot was fined, in April 1570, the excommunication from Rome which finally and completely forced the English Roman Catholics out of the National Church was promulgated in England. The sentence held in suspense by Popes Paul IV. and Pius IV. was launched by Pope Pius V., and Elizabeth was declared excommunicate and her subjects absolved from their allegiance; she was further anathematised as a heretic and pretended queen, and her tenure of the Crown declared null and void.

"We do out of the fulness of our apostolic power, declare the aforesaid Elizabeth, being heretic and a favourer of heretics, and her adherents in the matters aforesaid to have incurred the sentence of anathema and to be cut off from the unity of the Body of Christ."

The anathema of the Church was and is looked upon as an awful thing by Roman Catholics; it is feared by Protestants because of the devilish malice it lets loose upon the excommunicated, for the Canon Law of the Roman Church expresses the mind of the Church clearly enough, and history has marked the pages with bloody fingers. "We judge that they are not murderers who, burning with zeal for their Catholic Mother against the excommunicated, should happen to kill one of them." (Can. Excomm. 47, Cans. xxiii. qu v.)

In 1572 the Pope and his Cardinals went solemnly to Church and sang a *Te Deum* of thanksgiving for the Massacre of St. Bartholomew,

"Queen, Prelatist, and Puritan" 63

when the excommunicate Huguenots were butchered in the streets of Paris.

In 1580 Philip of Spain and Cardinal Granvelle issued their infamous "Ban" against the anathematised William the Silent. "We expose him as an enemy of the human race; if any of our subjects or any stranger should be found to rid us of this pest, dead or alive, we will cause to be delivered to him the sum of twenty-five thousand crowns in gold. If he have committed any crime however heinous we promise to pardon him, and if he be not already noble, we will ennoble him for his valour."

Gerard, the murderer of William the Silent, craved forgiveness and absolution from His Holiness because "he was about to keep company with heretics," and went about his odious work without one single thought except that by this "ridding of the pest" he would win paradise and be immortalised as a champion of the Holy Mother Church.

In May a fanatic named Felton (since declared a martyr of the cause of Christ and beatified by Pope Leo XIII. in 1887) affixed a copy of the bull to the door of the Bishop of London's palace. It created a tremendous excitement throughout the kingdom; a law was immediately passed making it high treason "to declare the Queen to be Heretic, Schismatick, Tyrant, Infidel and Usurper, to publish or put in use the Pope's bulls, to be reconciled to the Church of Rome, or to receive absolution by virtue of them."

Protestations of loyalty were signed all over England, "That Queen Elizabeth my sovereign lady, now reigning in England, is rightfully and ought to be and continue Queen, and lawfully beareth the Imperial Crown, notwithstanding any act or sentence that any Pope or Bishop has done or given or can do or give, and that if any Pope or other say or judge to the contrary, whether he say it as Pope, or howsoever, he erreth and affirmeth, holdeth and teacheth error."

In April 1571 the feelings of alarm and distrust rose almost to panic height by the discovery of the intrigues of the Italian banker, Ridolfi, who, with the Duke of Norfolk on the one hand and Alva on the other, was arranging for the landing of 6000 veteran Spanish cut-throats in England.

The plotters in England were arrested and executed in 1572.

Parliament was summoned in April, and great hopes were entertained by all sections of the Puritans that some pronounced legislation would be enacted in their favour. It was expected from the known state of the country that there would be a strong Puritan representation in the Commons, and as a matter of fact this proved to be the case.

Hallam says: "It is agreed on all hands and is quite manifest that the Puritans predominated in the House of Commons" (*Cons. His.*, note, chap. iv.). Gardiner writes: "The House of Lords wanted her to go backwards, to declare Mary her successor and to restore the Mass. The House of Commons wanted her to go forwards, to marry and have children of her own, and to alter the Prayer Book in a Puritan direction. Her temporising policy had naturally strengthened the Calvinism of the Calvinistic clergy. If Roman Catholics were to be kept out of the House of Commons, there was nothing to be done but to favour the election of Puritans, or at least those who had a leaning to Puritanism."

When Parliament met in the spring of 1571, the

Puritan strength of it was soon made manifest. Mr. Strickland introduced his Church Reform Bill, and supported it with a speech in which he showed how the Prayer Book might advantageously be altered without endangering any fundamental principle. A committee was appointed to consider the matter, and amongst other names that of Sir Thomas Lucy of Warwickshire appears (*D'Ewe's Journal*, 156). Again, on the question "touching the Bill against priests disguising themselves in serving-men's apparel," Lucy is on the committee; and in another Bill which was sent up to the Lords on May 6th "for coming to Church and receiving Communion," his name appears.

The most important Bill, however, which received the Royal Assent May 29th, 1571, was one which was recognised as a distinct favouring of the Puritans, and which implicitly acknowledged the validity of presbyterial ordination. It was called "An Act for Ministers of the Church to be of sound religion, or for Reformation of disorders in the Ministers of the Church."

Travers successfully pleaded the Statute in defence of his presbyterial ordination at Antwerp, and Archbishop Grindal regulated his practice by it when he licensed John Morrison, a Scottish Presbyterian, to ministerial work in England.

When the Session came to an end the Puritan outlook was decidedly brighter, although as yet none of the deeper questions had been dealt with; 1572 would bring them into line for settlement one way or the other.

"The future character of the Church of England was the real question at issue. Should the Reformed Church of England expand itself, and generously, or rashly it might be, cast itself on the affections of the people, and adapt itself to the growing passion for religious teaching, a passion which it might hope to lead and which it was wicked and insane to attempt to quench? This was one alternative. On the other hand, should it risk all hazards, resist every innovation and subdue by authority rather than conciliate by gentleness and love? In a word, should the Church be made more popular or more imperious?" (Marsden, *Puritans*, 109).

This was the problem which was agitating England. Deputations were sent up to London from counties and boroughs, and the opening of Parliament in 1572 was awaited with keenest interest. Alderman John Shakespeare, if one may judge by the chamberlains' reports of January 1571, was taking an active part in the discussions before Parliament, for several sums of money are recorded as being paid over to him; and if our assumption be correct, this money was for his travelling expenses to London and back. Altogether the sum of £VI was paid over at sundry times, the usual travelling expenses being XXs.

"*Jan.* 1571. Item, allowance of money delyvered to Mr. Shaxpere at sundrie times, £VI."

Thomas Barber and Nicholas Barneshurst were the borough chamberlains, and on September 5th, 1571, Adrian Quyney, whom we have seen in office in the strongly Protestant first year of Elizabeth, was again made bailiff, and John Shakespeare continued to hold a high position in the post of chief alderman.

It is worth while here to note the significant conjunction of names: Adrian Quyney is bailiff, John Shakespeare, chief alderman, John Wheler is an alderman and Thomas Barber and Nicholas

"Queen, Prelatist, and Puritan"

Barneshurst are chamberlains. Now, whenever we have seen these men occupying positions of influence in the Council, there have been undeniable evidences of strong Puritan feeling manifesting itself against Roman Catholicism.

Quyney was first mayor under Elizabeth; Shakespeare and Wheler were the active workers in the old Chapel renovations when the cross was torn down, the rood-loft destroyed, and the images and pictures defaced; they were the chief movers in the severe prosecution of Robert Perrot, and, as we shall show later, took a strong attitude of opposition in movements directed against the Puritans. Is it not significant that Shakespeare, Wheler, Barber, and Barneshurst are included as persistent Recusants in the return made by Sir Thomas Lucy in 1592, when the enactments against nonconforming Puritans were at their height?

What do we find here to be among the first official acts of Adrian Quyney and John Shakespeare? The Record is so conclusive that it only needs to be given to show its importance in our line of argument.

Within a month of Quyney's election, the following was passed:—

> "Yt is agreed at this Hall by the Balie, Aldermen, and capital burgeses herein assembled that Mr. Adrian Queny, now balye of the boroughe above seid, should sell the copes and vestements here under wrytten and thereof to yeld accompt of all suche money as shall receive for the same to the seid Chamber.
>
> "Imprimis, one suit of blew velvytt vestements, being thre in number.
>
> "Item, one sute of red velvytt, thre in number.
>
> "Item, one sute of whyt damaske, thre in number.
>
> "Item, ij coopes of tauny velvytt.
>
> "Item, j cope of whyte damask.
>
> "Item, j cope of blew velvytt.
>
> "Item, ij stoles and iij for the handes."

There can be only one interpretation to this most interesting Record, and that is, that this sale of the vestments (one of the cardinal points in the Puritan agitation) is part of that vigorous anti-papist policy which began with the chief magistracy of Quyney and was continued by John Shakespeare, and that it forms a suitable climax in that it is the sweeping away of what a Puritan would term "the last relics of the Amorites."

If this is not the action of Puritans, in what category are we to place John Shakespeare and

"Queen, Prelatist, and Puritan"

his friends? In the face of the Recusancy Return it is impossible to include them in the ranks of Queen's Churchmen; and if we ascribed their doings to extreme fervour in the Reformed religion, those very actions would be sufficient to stamp them Puritan. Nor can we after our study of their official acts number them among the Roman Catholics. Indeed, the question immediately suggests itself, By what abuse of charity could the Roman Catholic Church consider as her faithful sons men who denied their religious faith, shirked their responsibilities, took oaths to maintain a grievous schism, ranked themselves with the active persecutors of their brethren, and not only took service under a perjured, illegitimate, and excommunicated sovereign, but made themselves conspicuous by unswerving fidelity to her? It has been urged that the fact of their names being returned as Recusants is sufficient evidence of their Roman Catholicism; but they were returned as *refraining* from church attendance. Is it likely that men who had acted in defiance of every principle of their Church rather than be numbered among their suffering Papist brethren, would persistently expose themselves to imprisonment and death for the comparatively trifling matter of church attendance? Would men who had so grievously disgraced their Catholicism by shameful betrayal, have stopped short on the score of church attendance? It is almost absurd to think so, and therefore once again the only reasonable conclusion is, that John Shakespeare and his colleagues were not dishonest knaves and hypocrites, Papist or Prelatist, but that they were firmly, consistently, and persistently Puritan; and with this view the various events of their lives fall naturally into place, and we get an interesting picture of a sturdy group of Puritans working strenuously in the country borough of Stratford for what they would term liberty of conscience, but which meant fine, imprisonment, and death to their Roman Catholic fellow-countrymen. It was a narrow view, but in the main it was the Protestant view of Elizabeth's day.

In January 1572 a complimentary dinner was given by the borough to Sir Thomas Lucy, Sir Fulke Greville, Mr. Clement Throgmorton, and Mr. Goodeare, who had just returned from London. The expenses of this festive hobnobbing were met

"*Queen, Prelatist, and Puritan*" 73

by subscription; and one notes the pathos or irony of the situation in the words of the Record, which tells us that the persecuted "Mr. Perrot by the hands of Richard Woodward sends his contribution (xvs.) towards the charges of the dinner."

It is characteristic of both Quyney and Shakespeare that the persecution is aimed at the purse, for each worthy alderman was of that thrifty disposition which feels keenly any attack on the financial quarter.

Six days later, January 18th, 1572, a light is thrown upon the evident value of John Shakespeare's civic and political activity.

"At thys Hall yt is agreed by the asent and consent of the Aldermen and burgesses aforesaid that Mr. Adrian Queney now balyf and Mr. John Shakespere shall at Hillarii term next ensueing deale in the affayres concerninge the commonwealthe of the boroughe aforeseid accordinge to their discrecions. Yt ys lykwise agreed at this Hall that Mr. Thomas Barber, one of the Chamberlins of the said borough shal deliver to Mr. Baylif aforesaid at the seid Hillarii term the above wryten at London £vi."

The Hilary term came, and Puritan England sent up its representatives to make earnest efforts for greater reforms in the Church; Stratford, in addition to its Parliamentary representatives, sent up Shakespeare, Quyney, and Barber.

But the hopes of the Puritans were doomed to disappointment. Sir Peter Wentworth, who had introduced two Bills which were designed to cut away certain ceremonies and bring the English Reformation nearer the Geneva pattern, was arrested for "certain undutiful and irreverent words," and sent by order of the Queen to the Tower; and the Commons received a message "that henceforth no Bills concerning religion be received in this House until the same had been first considered and liked by the clergy."

Elizabeth had shown more of her intentions than was prudent for the time being, but the fearful news of the 24th August made her once more act so as to remove any Puritan alienation. The massacre on St. Bartholomew's day sent a thrill of indignant horror through the heart of Protestant Europe. The Queen put the whole Court into mourning, and received with haughtiest

"Queen, Prelatist, and Puritan"

coldness the explanation of Charles of France by the French Ambassador. And yet she did not break with France, and even allowed the rumour to be renewed which linked her name in marriage with that of the Duke of Alençon (afterwards Duke of Anjou).

Thus repulsed in Parliament, Puritan attention became directed to spiritual reformation within the Church as constituted, and a desire was manifested to make the best of the forms they had got. Religion had reached a very low ebb, the Lord's day was greatly profaned, Common Prayers were not frequented, many people, according to the Bishop of Worcester, "did not hear a sermon in seven years, or I might even say in seventeen." With the exception of the Puritan clergy, the ministers of the Church were a disgrace to their calling. Froude, who was no Puritan, says: "It would have fared ill with England had there been no hotter blood there than filtered in the sluggish veins of the officials of the Establishment. There was needed an enthusiasm fiercer far to encounter the revival of Catholic fanaticism; and if the young Puritans, in the heat and glow of their convictions, snapped their traces and flung off their harness, it was they after all who saved the Church which attempted to disown them" (vol. ix. 55 ch.).

In order to deal with the prevailing spiritual deadness, conferences for prayer and Bible instruction were established in ten dioceses. They were widely attended and were in no sense the outcome of a sectarian spirit; but they were put down by order of the Queen, and a proclamation was soon issued strictly commanding all men in authority to enforce with all severity and diligence the Act of Uniformity, neither favouring nor dissembling with anyone.

"All who shall be found non-conformable in the smallest matter shall be immediately apprehended and cast into prison; all who shall forbear coming to the Common Prayer and receiving the Sacraments according to the said Book shall be immediately prosecuted and punished; and all who shall in private houses or in public assemblies use any other rites of Common Prayer and administration of Sacraments, or shall maintain in their houses any persons guilty of these things, shall

"Queen, Prelatist, and Puritan"

be punished with the greatest severity" (*Sparrowe's Collection*, 169, 170). In order to carry out the penal laws against Papists and nonconforming ministers, commissioners were appointed in every shire, and in 1573 a form of subscription was drawn up for the laity, wherein the parishioner, after acknowledging the Queen to be Chief Governor of the Church under Christ and accepting the Prayer Book, adds: "And whereas I have absented myself from my parish Church and have refused to join with the congregation in publick prayer and in receiving the Sacrament according to the public order set down, I am right sorry for it and pray that this my fault may be pardoned, and I do promise that henceforth I will frequent my parish Church. And to witness this my promise I do hereunto willingly subscribe my name." The meshes of persecution were being drawn more closely around the Puritan, but as yet there was little cause to fear; the administration of the law had not been given into the hands of any vigorous opponent of Puritanism, so that the possibilities of a persecution exceeding that of the Roman Catholics was hardly dreamed of. But the cloud no bigger than the man's hand had appeared, and the Queen had on numerous occasions expressed her determination to root out Puritanism.

In 1575 affairs were quietly progressing in Stratford, John Wheler had again accepted the position of bailiff, and Alderman John Shakspeare is marked as one of the most regular attenders of the Council meetings. He had lately purchased from Edmond Hall two properties adjoining or near to the house he occupied in Henley Street, and from various entries it is clear that his business schemes were prospering, and that he was considered to be one of the most influential men of the town. His children were growing up around him, and his son William, now a scholar of the Grammar School, under the tuition of the well-known Thomas Hunt (afterwards deprived curate of Luddington), was laying the foundation of that scholarship which was destined to enrich so greatly the intellectual heritage of the world. So far the influences which went to form the budding character of the lad were those of the sylvan beauties of his own sweet county of Warwick; but the fiery discipline and strenuous thought which gave to the world a Spenser, a Milton, and a Bunyan were also destined to have their share in the moulding of his own character, and to make him realise in the depths of his own soul the intensity of those ideals which marked the greatest movement of our island story. The Puritanism which gave us Spenser, Milton, and Bunyan was not to pass over the great heart of William Shakespeare and leave it untouched and uninspired.

III

The Alleged Poverty of John Shakespeare

CHAPTER III

THE ALLEGED POVERTY OF JOHN SHAKESPEARE

THE year 1577 marked a new era in Elizabeth's dealing with the Puritans, and by a strange coincidence it marked also what has been considered the serious decline of John Shakespeare's fortune. We now approach that period in his life which has always presented most difficulty to his biographers. No matter how smoothly the voyage of their story has run on up to this point, henceforward it is bound in shallows and in miseries. It is easy to understand how that the life becomes inexplicable to biographers, who hedge themselves in on the one side by a presumed Roman Catholicism, and on the other by a theory of deep poverty. Halliwell Phillipps may be taken as representative when he says: "The conflict of evidences now becomes so exceedingly perplexing that it is hardly possible to reconcile them." If our argument so far has been correct respecting the strong Puritanism of John Shakespeare, it is only to be expected that the year 1577 would mark the beginning of a series of difficulties for him as it did for other Puritans. Active persecution in Warwickshire was initiated under the energetic leadership of Whitgift, who was afterwards promoted to the See of Canterbury, and the Courts of Star Chamber and High Commission made the life of the Puritan no less hunted than that of his Papist brother. Elizabeth had begun the second stage of the conflict by suppressing the Prophesyings: "Be vigilant," she wrote from her Manor of Greenwich on the 7th May, with that domineering tone she was apt to use to her divinely-appointed bishops, "lest we be forced to make some example of reforming of you according to your deserts." This blunt message won unwilling compliance from many bishops and drew a letter from Grindal, Archbishop of Canterbury, to the effect that the Exercises were useful spiritual agencies and ought to be continued. An Order of Star Chamber confined the Primate to his residence, and he was

Alleged Poverty of John Shakespeare 85

sequestrated from all archiepiscopal functions for six months. He never regained the Queen's favour, and his sequestration was continued until about a year from his death.

Spenser, in the *Shepherd's Calendar*, refers to him when he writes:

> "She weened the shell-fish to have broke
> But therewith bruized *his* brain;
> So now astonied with the stroke
> He lies in lingering payne."

The Queen's action was not misconstrued by the Puritans; they read its meaning clearly. Edward Deering, who was afterwards arrested for Puritanism, lost all Court favour about this time by making use of the following illustration before the Queen. "When Her Majesty was under persecution," said he, "her motto was 'Tanquam ovis,' but now it might be 'Tanquam indomita Juvenca' as an untamed heifer." How far he was justified may be judged from the Queen's remark to the French Ambassador in 1579, to the effect that "she would maintain the religion she was crowned in and baptized in; and would suppress the papistical religion, that it should not grow; but that she would root out Puritanism and the favourers thereof" (*Strype's Annals*, ii. p. 568). In order to carry out this intention the bishops were warned to be on the alert, justices of the peace were instructed, a special staff of inquisitors organised, and all the machinery of the Star Chamber made ready. Before long the prisons were full of godly ministers of the gospel and Puritan laymen. So many men were arrested that petitions began to flow in from all parts,— London, Essex, Lancashire, Warwickshire, Norfolk, Cheshire, and Cornwall,—and complaints against the vexatious character of the prosecutions were received from all over the land. " The conduct of the commissioners," writes Neal, "was high and imperious, their under officers were ravenous and greedy of grain: the fees of the Court were exorbitant, so that if an honest Puritan fell into their hands he was sure to be half ruined before he got out, even though he was cleared of the charge. The commissioners treated those that came before them neither like men nor Christians."

" The messenger of the Court was paid by the mile," corroborates Brooks, "and the fees were

Alleged Poverty of John Shakespeare 87

exorbitant which the prisoner must satisfy before he is discharged. The method of proceeding was dilatory and vexatious; if the prisoner was dismissed he was almost ruined with the charges and bound in a recognizance to appear again whensoever the Court should send for him."

Warwickshire was under the ecclesiastical jurisdiction of Whitgift. He had the appointing of the justices of the peace also, as the State Papers of Worcestershire for 1580 show, for authority had been given whereby the appointments were left to the discretion of the bishop, "and such others as the bishop shall think meet" runs the record (State Papers, Eliz., Worcester 1580). And concerning the county of Warwick, Strype corroborates this testimony in his life of Whitgift, by quoting (p. 188), in reference to the nominations for justices, "such as the Lord Bishop shall think meet." With a bench of justices nominated and approved by a bitter and persecuting Prelatist, it is manifest that the nonconforming party would not be allowed to rest quietly. Froude dismisses Whitgift with the caustic judgment: "Of all types of human beings who were generated by the

English Reformation, men like Whitgift are the least interesting. There is something in the constitution of the Establishment which forces them into the administration of it; yet but for the statesmen to whom they refused to listen, and the Puritans whom they endeavoured to destroy, the old religion would have come back on the country like a returning tide. The Puritans would have furnished new martyrs; the statesmen, through good and evil, would have watched over liberty, but the High Church clergy would have slunk back into conformity or dwindled to their proper insignificance."

John Shakespeare was a man who held considerable property; and an owner of real estate gives hostages to persecution. He was well known as a public man of no mean capacity, and his name had been identified with movements of religious reform. We have seen how vitally interested he was in all that concerned the borough, therefore it is to the highest degree unlikely that a man of his capacity and wide activities could have been untouched by the stirring religious events of the year. In those days politics and religion went hand-in-hand, usually religion was the essence of politics. But Alderman Shakespeare was also a man who was careful of his money; he seldom let his heart overcome his head, as witness his steady cautious givings to the poor, and he knew how to make a good bargain. In time of storm, then, it is to be anticipated that he would take steps to make his property secure. As a prudent man he would foresee the danger and turn aside, although as a Puritan he would not be likely to forsake what seemed to him to be the plain path of duty. And here it is well to remember that the Reformer of Elizabeth's day was not the caricature some writers assume him to be: "Little Bethels" and pious saints of the Stiggins type were utterly and entirely unknown in that day; the men who held most tenaciously to the Puritan ideals were English gentlemen and yeomen of highest Christian character; the clergymen were all University men of high distinction, able to defend with widest and soundest scholarship the views they advocated, and always adorning their doctrine with earnest, godly lives. The snuffling hypocrite was a fungus growth upon Puritanism, and too frequently the product of Cavalier potations and imaginings or the extravagances of an arid and debased sectarianism.

From the year 1576 John Shakespeare's attendances at the Council begin to be very irregular. He seems to have lost all interest in civic life, and only attends when business of a special nature is under consideration.

On January 29th, 1578, a subscription was levied upon members of the Council for the equipment of some soldiers.

"At this Hall yt ys agreed that every Alderman except suche underwryten excepted shall paye towardes the furniture of thre pikemen, ij billmen and one archer vjs. viijd. and every burgese except suche underwryten excepted shall pay iijs. iiijd.

> Mr Plumley, vs.
> Mr. Shaxpere, iijs. ivd. } Aldermen."
> John Walker, ijs. vjd.

It is difficult to say why there should be any exception made in these cases, or why Alderman John Shakespeare is allowed to get off by paying a burgess's subscription. It has been explained that perhaps at this time John Shakespeare was living outside the borough boundaries; but the assess-

Alleged Poverty of John Shakespeare 91

ment is on individuals rather than on householders, so this suggestion does not help very much. But in any case this fact does not necessarily imply poverty, for as a trader John Shakespeare's credit would be worth more to him than the 3s. 4d. assessment; and the way in which the matter is recorded does not seem to indicate that the three were accepting anything that was not perfectly legitimate and straightforward.

Again, on November 19th, 1578, another subscription is made for the poor. "Yt ys ordered that every Alderman shall paye weekly towardes the releef of the poor IIIjd. savinge John Shaxpeare and Robert Bratt who shall not be taxed to paye anythinge."

It has been questioned whether this John Shaxpeare is Mr. Alderman Shakespeare or not, and in any case fourpence a week either one way or the other does not amount to much as an argument of poverty, but the ominous announcement which follows this exemption in the Record is far more important.

"Item, it is ordened at this Hall that every Alderman and burgess that hath made default not comminge to this Hall accordinge to the order shall paye their amerciament." It will be remembered how severe the enactments were which were passed by the Council when John Shakespeare was bailiff, in order to enforce attendance. There would be men on the Council who would remember how rigorously Robert Perrot's fine had been enforced, and it was not likely that the Puritan would be spared now the Prelatist was having the upper hand. If John Shakespeare by his *poverty* was escaping a levy of fourpence a week for poor relief, he was also by his *intentional absence* from the Court laying himself open to the infliction of a heavy and concurrent fine. The Record shows us that the "amerciament" would have to be paid. And there is no doubt that John Shakespeare had sufficient personal property and real estate to make his prosecution worth taking up. Commissioners, spies, and informers were only too glad to snare a man whose possessions made him worth the plucking; and even though his colleagues on the Council were inclined to be lenient, the Ecclesiastical Commissioners were not likely to be so merciful.

Alleged Poverty of John Shakespeare

In the beginning of 1580 Alderman John Shakespeare undoubtedly held the following possessions:—

(*a*) The property purchased from Edward West in 1556, situated in Henley Street.

(*b*) A house in Greenhill Street, by the end of the Rother Street.

(*c*) The property bought in 1575 from Edmund Hall, situated in Henley Street.

(*d*) Reversionary interests in the freehold estate of the "Asbies" in Wilmcote, consisting of house, appurtenances, and about 60 acres of land, and in the property at Snitterfield, an estate of over 100 acres. In 1570 he held under Clopton a freehold and 14 acres called "the Ingon," a short distance out of Stratford, for which he paid eight pounds a year rent; it may have passed out of his tenancy before 1579, but it is instructive to note the rental paid by him for 14 acres, about eighteen months after a writ had been issued against him.

Now, assuming that John Shakespeare was a Puritan, these outlying estates would be a constant source of anxiety to him, because they always presented a vulnerable point of attack to that Court which he feared most, namely, the Bishops. Within the borough, influential friends might possibly shield him, but beyond its confines Whitgift reigned supreme. It was only to be expected that the Wilmcote and Snitterfield estates would be doubly valuable to him because of their tender associations,—they were a portion of his wife's inheritance. How then could he best safeguard their possession? The Lansdowne MSS. gives us an insight into the methods adopted by Papist and Puritan Recusants for the protection of their property. A trusted man was usually chosen to be the purchaser or lease-holder; and while the documents were drawn up in strictly legal form, sometimes exaggerated to the point of confusion (for the spies of the Courts were very keen), it was an understood thing that when the storm blew over, or a change in government and religion occurred, the estates would be handed back to the true owner. It will easily be seen that this was only a choice between two evils, for everything depended upon the integrity of the receiver of the property; and

Alleged Poverty of John Shakespeare 95

the very strictness with which the legal documents were drawn up placed the Puritan or Papist in hopeless case if his claim were disputed. Very far-seeing men drew up conditional documents which they retained as a security, but few receivers would accept this evidence of distrust in their own *bona-fides*, so the Recusant was compelled to take his chances.

"The Recusants convey all their lands and goods to friends of theirs before their convictions, and are relieved by those that have the same lands" (Lan. MSS., 153, 232.)

In 1579 Agnes Arden, the widow of the Roman Catholic Robert Arden and holder of the Snitterfield estate, was spoken of as being "aged and impotent," and it was evident that the property must soon fall into John Shakespeare's hands, as representing his wife, Mary Arden. Agnes Arden died December 1580. She had, however, on the 21st May, in the second year of Elizabeth, entered into an agreement with her brother, Alexander Webbe, whereby she granted him a forty years' lease of the Snitterfield property.

"Unto the said Alexander Webbe for a terme

of fourtie years next and immediately following, fully to be completed and ended yff the said Agnes Arderne so long do lyve, yeldinge and paying therefor yearely during the said terme unto the said Agnes Arderne or her assignes, fourtie shillynges of lawful money of Englande, to be payd at two termes of the yere by equall portions."

Alexander Webbe died in 1573, after appointing as one of the overseers of his will his friend and kinsman, John Shakespeare of Stratford. Robert Webbe presumably received the benefit of the lease, for on October 15th, 1579, while all England was in a ferment over the exciting incidents which followed the Puritan outburst against the Queen's intended marriage with the Duke of Anjou, John Shakespeare quietly entered into an agreement with him in regard to the future of the property, for it was manifest that the aged and impotent Agnes Arden could not live very long, and therefore John Shakespeare, as heir-at-law through his wife, must needs be consulted. The document is a mystifying one to the non-legal mind, and can only be fairly appraised by men well posted in the conveyances of Elizabeth's day, but certain

Alleged Poverty of John Shakespeare 97

features strike even non-legal students as peculiar. The wearisome fulness, the curious entries of fine, forfeiture, etc., and the accompanying conditional documents all make up what Halliwell Phillipps terms a very curious transaction. Alexander Webbe paid a merely nominal rental of "fourtie shillynges a year" for a farm of over 100 acres, —certainly a lease on the most favourable terms possible, and evidently a nominal payment from a brother to a sister. How does Robert Webbe fare at the hands of the new owner, John Shakespeare? As well, if not better than the preceding leaseholder, "for and in consideration of the somme of foure poundes of goode and lawfull Englishe money by the aforesaid Robert Webbe, the property etc. maye and shall lawfully and rightfully come be and remayne unto thaforesaid Robert Webbe, his heires and assignes according to the true tenour and effecte of the graunte thereof before made in these presentes, free, cleire, and voyde, or otherwise well and sufficiently saved harmlesse by the foresaid John Shakespeare and Marye his wyeffe, their heires and the heires of eyther of them, and their assignes of and from all and singular bargains, sales, feoffments, grauntes, intayles, joyntures, dowars, leases, willes, uses, rent charges, rent sects, arrerages of rent, recognizaunce, statute marchant and of the staple, obligacions, judgements, executions, condempnacions, yssues, fynes, amercements, intrusions, forfeitures, alienacyons without lycens, etc."

Accompanying this was a still more peculiar conditional document which was sealed and delivered in the presence of Nycholas Knooles, vicar of Auston, whereby in certain contingencies "this present obligacion to be utterlye voyde and of none effect or ells to stande, remayne, and be in full power, strengthe, force and vertue." (See Hall. Phil., vol. ii. 182, 49 for full copies.)

Now, in whatever light we may regard this agreement, whether as a genuine sale or as a contingent lease (like the lease entered into by Alexander Webbe in 1569 with one Thomas Stringer, the witness thereof being John Shakespeare), at least two important considerations claim our attention. In the first place, it is clear that as Alexander Webbe died in 1573, that is, six years before the date under notice, that therefore Robert Webbe

Alleged Poverty of John Shakespeare

was not immediately stepping into the dead man's shoes, nor does he make the agreement with the present holder of the property, Agnes Arden, who was still alive on October 15th, 1579, when the arrangement was made. It is manifest that both sides were providing against any contingency which might arise in reference to John Shakespeare *before* the reversionary interests had actually fallen into his hands. The property was safeguarded against any "condempnacions, yssues, fynes, amercements, intrusions, forfeitures, alienacyons," by being vested in other hands; and the spies of the Ecclesiastical Courts, ever ready to swoop down upon the property of Puritans, would find when the tidings of Agnes Arden's death was brought to them, that Robert Webbe (presumably a safe man) was in possession. And secondly, the propounders of the destitution theory adduce this transaction as an evidence of the pressing needs of Alderman Shakespeare at this time, and say that the overwhelming nature of these pecuniary difficulties may be understood from the fact that a husband is being forced to part with what ought to have been his dearest possession, namely, his wife's heritage.

But if Alderman John Shakespeare, after waiting many years for this property to fall into his hands, disposed of it to Robert Webbe for the "somme of foure poundes of goode and lawfull Englishe money," his act would be that of an "incapable" and not of a "poor" man. The transaction might with greater justice have been made to buttress up a theory of insanity. There is nothing of the aptitude of the business man about it, and from all we know of John Shakespeare we have no cause to doubt the keenness of his commercial instincts nor the quality of his mercantile abilities; but to sell a valuable property and his wife's heritage for half the yearly rental he paid for fourteen acres at the "Ingon" would be a contradiction of his whole life. And how could it possibly be the action of a poor man who was striving to extricate himself from a maze of financial difficulties? A man in straits would naturally make the most of such an opportunity to secure the best possible bargain. To fling away the estate for a trifle would be an act of insanity, or, if more charitably construed, might be taken as the action of a very *rich* man, who was anxious to perform an act of grace towards a poor relative.

Alleged Poverty of John Shakespeare 101

The only satisfactory explanation seems to be on the lines of our argument, that it was a contingent lease on the most favourable terms in order to safeguard the property for Alderman John Shakespeare, who was living under the dread of alienation for recusancy.

Regarding the Wilmcote property, the "Asbies," the way is clearer, because the documentary evidence is that which was laid before the Court of Chancery some twenty years after the events had transpired, when John Shakespeare was claiming the estate from the Lambarts, whom he accused of swindling.

In the will of Robert Arden the bequest ran: "I geve and bequeth to my youngste dowghter Marye all my lande in Willmcote, cawlide Asbies, and the crop upon the ground sown and tyllede as hit is." Near Wilmcote, at Barton-on-the-Heath, Joan Arden, sister of Mary, lived with her husband, Edmond Lambart. They were to all appearance on good terms with their Stratford relatives, in spite of the fact that Mary had received by far the largest share of the inheritance, for the name Joan had already been given to John Shakespeare's little daughter, and in 1580 the youngest son had been called "Edmond" after his uncle.

With this brother-in-law John Shakespeare entered into an agreement whereby, for the payment of £40, Lambart was to enter into possession of the "Asbies,"—at that time evidently an unoccupied property,—and remain until the money was refunded to him at the Feast of St. Michael Archangel 1580. It was expressly stated by John Lambart, the son, in his evidence later, that a "conditional privisoe" was in the deed. So far the property was safeguarded until Michaelmas 1580, but there is ground to infer that John Shakespeare had a shrewd suspicion that Edmond Lambart felt sore about the matter of the inheritance, and that he might play him a knave's trick, for in the Hilary term of the same year 1579 he granted a twenty-one years' lease of the same property to one George Gibbes, dating from the Feast of Michaelmas 1580, that is, *the very day on which Edmond Lambart's lien on the property would be removed by the payment of the £40.* The terms were exceedingly favourable to Gibbes, being "the moiety of one quarter of wheat and the moiety of one quarter of barley"

Alleged Poverty of John Shakespeare   103

(Stratford Record). The arrangement does not seem to have been carried out so far as George Gibbes was concerned, but that his interest continued is seen by a fine levied on the Asbies in 1597, wherein George Gibbes transfers his right to Thomas Webbe and Humphrey Hooper. Robert Webbe was the trusted holder of the Snitterfield property, Thomas Webbe was to safeguard John Shakespeare's interest in the "Asbies."

"Thomam Webbe et Humfridum Hooper, querentes, et Johannem Shakespere et Mariam uxorem ejus et Georgium Gybbes, deforciantes etc."

But the scheme failed because of Edmond Lambart, for on September 29th, 1580, when Alderman Shakespeare paid his visit to the "Asbies" to pay over to his kinsman the £40 advanced on the property, Lambart refused to surrender the holding until certain other moneys had been forwarded. The agreement distinctly stipulated "that if the sum was payd before a certain day it should be void," but Lambart declined to hand over the property, and Alderman Shakespeare was forced to acquiesce.

Edmond Lambart died in 1589, and John

Shakespeare lodged a complaint against John Lambart, the son, succeeding to the estate, but nothing was done. It was not until November 24th, 1597, after the days of persecution were over, that the defrauded John Shakespeare dared fight the question in the Court of Chancery. He appealed, stating the transaction with Edmond Lambart, and pointing out how he (Lambart) had broken the agreement. "After which your seide orators did tender unto the saide Edmunde the sayd sum of fowertie pounds and desired that they might have agayne the sayd premisses accordinge to their agreement, which money he the sayde Edmunde then refused to receive, saying that he would not receive the same nor suffer your sayd orators to have the saide premisses agayne, unless they woulde paye unto him certayne other money which they did owe unto him for other matters."

John Lambart replied that John Shakspeare had not fulfilled the conditions agreed upon, and that therefore the estate on his father's death legally reverted to him, against which John Shakespeare urged in a further statement that on the Feast of

Alleged Poverty of John Shakespeare

St. Michael Archangel 1580 he had gone with the £40 to Edmond Lambart, and that the payment had been persistently refused; he further stated that his present appeal was not due to a desire to profit from the increased value of the property, as insinuated by John Lambart, but that it had come to his knowledge that the said Lambart was secretly selling portions of the estate, and that he was in illegal possession of documents of great importance which rightly belonged to the Shakespeares, "by reasone that certaine deeds and other evydences concerninge the premises and that of righte belong to your saide orators, are comme into the handes and possession of the sayde John, he wrongfully still keepeth and detaineth the possession of the sayde premisses." It is not clear how the matter ended finally; the chances are that John Lambart kept possession by reason of the documents having passed into his hands, but it is very plain that John Shakespeare never contemplated a transference of the property to Edmond Lambart. He was not a poor man when he made the agreement, for it was about the year 1575 ("he did enjoye the same for the space of three or four years"), a time of acknowledged prosperity with Alderman Shakespeare, and he was not destitute at Michaelmas 1580, or he would not have been able to offer the £40 to Lambart. Therefore the supporters of the "destitution" theory are once again forced from the position that poverty was the cause of these transactions. Neither side hints that a *sale* of the property was effected; and the fact that John Shakespeare accepted the £40 when he was well off, and had it in hand to repay when the date came round, is conclusive enough against the idea of financial difficulty. The estate was lost to the Shakespeares by a piece of sharp practice on the part of the Lambarts, a deceit which the keenness of the persecution of the Recusants rendered comparatively easy. In safeguarding himself against the possible attacks of the Ecclesiastical Courts, John Shakespeare was forced to trust to the good faith of a kinsman. He was betrayed by his dishonesty, and the calamity he dreaded was thus brought about. It was treachery from a quarter more or less suspected by himself, yet events had so transpired that he

Alleged Poverty of John Shakespeare

had found it impossible to transfer the property to the safer hands of Thomas Webbe. Lambart by his clever roguery thus lorded it over an estate which did not belong to him. It may be that there is a local reference in the somewhat unnecessary Induction to the *Taming of the Shrew*, where the angry landlord upbraids the rogue Sly.

Host. A pair of stocks, you rogue.
Sly. Y'are a baggage; the Slys are no rogues: Look in the Chronicles, we came in with Richard Conqueror.
Host. I know my remedy; I must go fetch the third-borough.
Sly. Third, or fourth, or fifth borough, *I'll answer him by law*: I'll not budge an inch, boy; let him come. [*Falls asleep.*

And again the same rogue says when he is acknowledged lord of the great estate and handsome house he awakes in—

"Call me not 'honour' nor 'lordship.' Am not I Christopher Sly, . . . *old Sly's son of Burton-heath.*"

William Shakespeare was without doubt behind his father in the suit against John Lambart to recover the property, and would feel keenly the treachery which deprived him of so valuable an estate. So whether this idea of a local reference be empty surmise or no, it is certain that the cap fitted the Lambarts of Barton Heath, and that from John Shakespeare's standpoint John Lambart was indeed "old Sly's son of Burton Heath."

ID

Active Persecution of Puritans

CHAPTER IV

ACTIVE PERSECUTION OF PURITANS AND JOHN SHAKESPEARE'S INCREASING DIFFICULTIES

IT was significant that Alderman John Shakespeare was anxiously endeavouring to safeguard his outlying possessions in the later months of the year 1579, for, as mentioned in the last chapter, this was a time of keen excitement in England because of the acute state of feeling aroused in the Puritan party by reason of the Queen's projected marriage with the brother of the monarch who was responsible for the massacre of the Huguenots in France on St. Bartholomew's black day. The Duke of Anjou had paid a visit to Elizabeth at Greenwich, and had been received with such significant marks of favour that the Queen's supposed Papist leanings had filled her Protestant subjects with deep apprehensions. The political outlook no doubt made Elizabeth inclined to play a deep game against her opponents, and statecraft necessitated an apparent alliance with France, but her subjects had not the statesman's knowledge of the case, and were consequently filled with dread. Hume says: "Spain was formidable, Scotland was uncertain, Ireland was prepared for rebellion, and seminary priests were everywhere disseminating treason and disaffection throughout the Queen's dominions." An alliance with France might possibly have commended itself to many politicians, but the murmurs of dissatisfaction against having "a Protestant body under a Popish head" culminated in a stirring pamphlet entitled "The Gaping Gulph in which England will be swallowed up by the French marriage," wherein the feelings of the extremer section of the Puritans found expression. Curiously enough, Warwickshire was closely interested in the author of the pamphlet, John Stubbe, the famous Puritan lawyer; who was brother-in-law to Thomas Cartwright, the friend of the Earls of Leicester and Warwick, and afterwards the leader of the Warwickshire Puritans. Stubbe was immediately arrested and sentenced to have

Active Persecution of Puritans

the guilty right hand struck off; waving the bleeding stump, he raised his hat with the left hand, and cried, "Long live the Queen." The agitation spread throughout the kingdom, and disturbances were reported from all parts. Puritan feeling expressed itself so strongly that the authorities took measures to keep the peace and repress any dangerous excitement. Additional soldiers were enlisted in the boroughs, and levies were ordered to be raised to overawe the Puritans. In Stratford the strong feeling aroused is sufficiently attested by the fact that a rate was levied for the equipment of additional pikemen, and special meetings of the Council were summoned in order to cope with the difficulty. Aldermen and councillors were divided, and it became necessary to issue threats of the enforcement of penalties in order to obtain an assembly. The whole Hall was proclaimed on one occasion, and several well-known aldermen were severely fined for non-attendance. Alderman John Shakespeare and Alderman John Wheler were the most prominent among them.

The rate was levied for the purpose of providing

arms and equipment for additional pikemen. John Shakespeare as a property owner was included in the levy, but his name is returned with a number of others as a defaulter. It was only a matter of a few shillings, but he allowed his name to be published as a defaulting alderman. That this is a case of refusal, and not of inability to pay, is sufficiently attested by the fact that the names of known well-to-do people are included in the list. Mr. Halliwell Phillipps, who accepts the general theory of John Shakespeare's poverty, says: "I cannot imagine that it shows anything further beyond the fact that he was rated as if he were a man of good property and styled 'Mr.' in very good company." It stands to reason that John Shakespeare could easily have afforded the few shillings required, for he was rated as a property owner, and therefore the fact of his known ability and possession of property was the reason why the levy was made upon him as a qualified ratepayer. Hence his non-payment was a refusal. We have seen that when the Roman Catholic rising in the north of England had to be put down with the strong hand, John Shakespeare was

Active Persecution of Puritans

the leading spirit in the Stratford Town Council, compelling all the burghers to rally to the support of the Queen's cause, and severely punishing Alderman Robert Perrot for his non-attendance at the meetings. Now, when it is a question of Puritan repression, we find him absolutely refusing to take any hand in the matter, and with his friend John Wheler laying himself open to all the penalties of non-compliance. Indeed the Puritan feeling of the town was so thoroughly aroused that all sections of the community seem to have taken the alarm. On July 15th the whole Council was proclaimed, and John Wheler was fined. "The woole hall to be proclaimed, Mr. Wheler hath made default not appearinge at this hall, according to this order, therefore to be amersed." Nor was the agitation confined to the borough itself, but from every village in the countryside Puritan sympathisers hastened to avow themselves on the Puritan side, every market cart which rolled into Stratford brought some excited Boanerges with it, and these rural sons of thunder brought weapons with them, so that when the tongue failed a keener edge might take part in the discussion. The

116 *Shakespeare : Puritan and Recusant*

Records are sufficiently plain on the matter. One resolution of Council of August 2nd, 1579, says:

"Hyt hys agreed this daye that proclamacyon be mayd to-moro in the Market place that all persons commyng to oure market, that they kepe the Quenes Majesties peace within the borrow, and that they leve ther wepons at ther innes, that all inhabytense to assyste the offycers in kepinge the peace in payne of imprisonment and they losse ther fredome" (Strat. Records, Book A).

On September 9th the usual Council meeting was called, but as only six aldermen and four burgesses attended, there was "No act donne at thys Hall for lacke of the Companye."

Numerous arrests were made. Sir Thomas Lucy and Sir William Catesby came into the borough as magistrates, and the old Town prison was fitted with new chains and staples to secure the prisoners. The picture of this stirring time is made complete for us in the accounts submitted in January 1581, when we have the following significant items:—

"Paid to Richard Hernbe for linckes and staples for the serjauntes to make fast their prisoners, xij d.

Active Persecution of Puritans

"Paid for wine that was given to Sir Thomas Lucy and Sir William Catesby, IIJs. IIIJd.

"Pottell of sack for the Justices, xvJd.

"Wine for the Justices, IJs."

All this meant active repression, and it was directed against the Puritans; indeed, from this date the hostility of the Queen and the Prelatic party towards Puritanism swept to its full height. The Parliament of 1580 began its deliberations smarting under a keen sense of humiliation by reason of the sharp reproof administered by the Queen on the occasion of the proposed meeting of the members of the House for the purpose of united prayer at the Temple Church, when Alvey the Puritan was master.

Hatton, the vice-chamberlain, conveyed the Queen's prohibition of the Assembly. "She did much admire," the ironical message ran, "the great rashness in that House, as to put in execution such an innovation without her privity and pleasure first made known to them."

The House acknowledged the error of daring to assemble for special prayer to the King of kings without the permission of the daughter of Henry

VIII., and proceeded soon afterwards, under the masterful force of the Queen, to pass a measure which tacked the Puritans to the Papists, and subjected them to the same penal laws. "All persons that do not come to church or chapel or other place where Common Prayer is said according to the Act of Uniformity, shall forfeit £20 a month to the Queen, being thereof lawfully convict, and suffer imprisonment till paid. Those that are absent for twelve months shall upon certificate made thereof unto the King's Bench, besides their former fine, be bound with two sufficient sureties in a bond of £200 for their good behaviour. Every schoolmaster that does not come to Common Prayer shall forfeit £10 a month, be disabled from teaching school, and suffer a year's imprisonment." A full conformity was further enjoined, and half-conformists, who evaded punishment by coming to the services when they were nearly over, were ordered to be specially looked after.

On September 23rd, 1583, Whitgift of Worcester was made Archbishop of Canterbury, and the persecutor of a diocese became the tyrant of a

Active Persecution of Puritans

kingdom—"there was no danger of *his* Grindalizing," as his biographer writes.

He brought a heart-whole subserviency to the wishes of the Queen, and received her exhortation "to restore the discipline of the Church, and the Uniformity established by Law, which, through the connivance of some Prelates, the obstinacy of the Puritans, and the power of some noblemen, is run out of square."

The first step was the famous Whitgift Test Articles, whereby the Archbishop sought to establish the principle that canons enacted by Convocation and assented to by the Crown were binding on all holding clerical office, even although such canons had not received the assent of Parliament. Having placed the Crown and Convocation above Constitutional Law, Whitgift was forced to create new machinery for the carrying out of unconstitutional enactments. This he did by forty-four High Commissioners, twelve of whom were to be bishops, and the rest chief officers of the Crown. Any three could act provided a bishop were present. They received unlimited powers of coercion, and were "to enquire from time to time during our pleasure as well by the oaths of twelve good and lawful men, as also by witnesses, and all other means and ways you can devise, of all offences, contempts, misdemeanours, done and committed contrary to the tenor of the said several Acts and Statutes, and also to enquire of all heretical opinions, seditious books, contempts, conspiracies, false rumour or talks, slanderous words or sayings contrary to the aforesaid laws."

"Also to take order that the penalties and forfeitures may be duly levied upon the goods, lands, and tenements of such offenders, by way of distress."

"Also to examine such person suspected *on their corporal oaths* for the better trial and opening of truth, and to punish those that refused the oath by fine or imprisonment *according to their discretions*."

We have underlined the passages of the Statute which especially reveal the malignant determination of the authorities to put down Puritan nonconformity. The clause "by all other means and ways you can devise" opened up the way for the rack and torture.

Active Persecution of Puritans 121

"According to their discretions" usurped the place of the usual formula, "according to the power and authority limited and appointed by the laws, ordinances, and Statutes of this Realm;" while the infamous "oath officio mero" by which a man might be made to condemn himself or others, or be punished by continuous fine and imprisonment, was a power exceeding that given to the Roman Inquisition in its worst days. Henry VIII. had repealed it, Elizabeth in her first year had declared it illegal, the Popes only allowed it in cases of heresy, Whitgift levelled it against every paltry misdemeanour.

The effect of the Test Articles upon responsible statesmen may be judged from the appeals of the Lords of the Council, Warwick, Leicester, Shrewsbury, Lord Charles Howard, Sir James Crofts, Sir Francis Walsingham, and many others.

The Lord Treasurer Burleigh protested in a letter dated July 15th, 1584: "I favour no sensual and wilful Recusant, but I conclude according to my simple judgment, that this kind of proceeding is too much favouring of the Romish Inquisition, and is a device rather to seek for offenders than to reform."

The voice of the country also made itself heard in petitions from county associations, from professors, clergymen, and laymen of all classes of the Protestant Church of England, who recognised that these wide-reaching powers were meant for the compulsion of those Protestants who were absenting themselves from their parish churches. Papists had throughout the Queen's reign been persecuted because of their adherence to Rome, but now Puritan Recusants were to be forced and harried into complete conformity.

It would have gone terribly hard with the Puritans in 1585 had not new intrigues on the part of the Jesuits in some measure withdrawn the attention of the authorities; and the cruel murder of William the Silent at Delft and sinister rumours from Spain united Englishmen, Puritan and Prelatist, into an association (confirmed by Parliament) pledged to defend Elizabeth and England from vengeful and fanatical intrigues.

The edge of the weapon was turned for the time being, but it remained in the hands of the High

Active Persecution of Puritans 123

Commissioners, and the dread of it lay like the fear of death on every village in England. Town councils were forced into co-operation with the local commissioners, ecclesiastical spies and informers were on the look-out for victims, the prisons were being filled with Puritans awaiting trial, many families were preparing to leave the old country altogether.

John Shakespeare had made a comfortable fortune and won a high position during the period when the laws against the Roman Catholics were being rigorously enforced; it is instructive to note the change that comes over his political and civic activity when the Puritan is being harried throughout the land. He avoids all legal controversies, ceases to attend the Council meetings, and finally allows his name to be struck off the rolls as an alderman. Before this he had absented himself from eighteen consecutive meetings of the Council, and only put in an appearance when an old friend, John Sadler, was about to be nominated for bailiff.

In 1582 his son William Shakespeare was married to Ann Hathaway.

In 1585 Thomas Cartwright, the famous Puritan leader and controversialist, returned from exile in Antwerp, and after a short imprisonment was made Warden of the Leycester Hospital in Warwick, a few miles from John Shakespeare's home. Here Sunday after Sunday he preached to large congregations drawn from the surrounding districts, and it is recorded that Puritans for twelve and even twenty miles left their parish churches to hear Cartwright preach

On January 19th, 1586, the writ upon which so much reliance is made as an evidence of poverty was issued against Alderman Shakespeare; it was returned to the Court with the note written across it "quod praedictus Johannes Shakspere nihil habet unde distringere potest habet." As we have pointed out, John Shakespeare would not be unaccustomed to writs in the course of his business transactions, and from his well-known legal adroitness would no doubt be able to prepare himself against distraint; at anyrate, he is still in possession of his Stratford property, and, as a recalcitrant alderman, evidently paying a heavy fine for persistent non-attendance at the Council, for, as

Active Persecution of Puritans 125

Halliwell Phillipps points out in reference to his absence, this implies rather the possession of abundant means than the lack of it. "This is not an evidence of falling off in circumstances, but rather the opposite, for it implies on the contrary the ability to pay the fines for non-attendance, for we cannot doubt if he had not paid them some notice would have appeared in the books."

In May, Alderman John Shakespeare is summoned as a juryman in an important case, and a few months later his official connection with the Stratford Council was brought to a close by the removal of his name for persistent non-attendance. His long absence had doubtless made it clear that he was hopelessly at variance with the repressive measures of the Council, and consequently his name was struck off.

"*Sept.* 6, 1586. At thys hall William Smythe and Richard Courte are chosen to be Aldermen in the places of John Wheler and John Shaxpere, for that Mr. Wheler doth desyre to be put out of the Companye and Mr. Shaxpere doth not come to the halles when they be warned nor hath not done of longe tyme."

And so the long and honourable career reached its climax in what was practically self-exclusion. Mr. Wheler had lost all heart for Council work, and Mr. Shakespeare was treating it with a silent contempt.

It is an easy solution of the problem to say that this abstention had its root in a deep poverty which made old associations painful and a position of influence irksome and contradictory. The easy-going critic of the "destitute theory" school finds the circumstances of Alderman Shakespeare's later days fit in wonderfully. What can be more conclusive? A man sells two valuable estates which ought to have had a high sentimental value, he is exempted from a certain subscription, he owes his relative Lambart money, he cannot pay a levy, he has a writ of distraint issued against him which is returned with the remark that he has nothing to distrain upon, he is put out of the Council and deprived of his office as alderman, and finally, as a ruined man and a bankrupt, his home is broken up and he is thrown into prison for debt. So runs the argument.

We have endeavoured to show what we believe

to be the correct and relative values of most of these incidents, and would point out several important considerations in this leaving of the Council. It is clear that so far as John Shakespeare was concerned he had *excluded himself* and practically resigned his office many months before the meeting in September 1586. Mr. John Wheler is excluded by the same resolution of the Council on his own request.

Again we have the two names together, the significant conjunction of which we have pointed out more than once. Were these worthy citizens *both* put out of the Council because of poverty? No one has yet attempted to show that John Wheler was a poor man at this or any other time; he was always spoken of in terms which imply the possession of ample properties, and is returned as an owner of real estate in various Exchequer returns; four years after this date, in 1590, he is recorded as an owner, and in the *same* Exchequer return, for the Survey of Properties, John Shakespeare is also mentioned as still holding the Henley Street property and its appurtenances. Why, then, is John Shakespeare, in spite of this fact, singled out to be the victim of misfortune and penury, and why is abject poverty accepted as the cause of the close of his civic career? We would remind theorists who find the "conflict of evidences so exceedingly perplexing that it is hardly possible to reconcile them," that the perplexity lies in their own theories and not in the facts themselves, and that the linking together of the names of John Shakespeare and John Wheler, still "worshipful men of property," is not because of poverty, but on account of that religious association which we have seen uniting them from the earliest years of Elizabeth, that Puritan sentiment which was now being cemented into closest fellowship by reason of the fierce persecution which was filling countless dungeons and graves and causing Englishmen to gaze with wistful longing across the wild waves of the Atlantic to where the New World offered religious freedom and liberty of conscience. Puritans in all parts of England were abstaining from attendance at the Halls "when they be summoned." It is an extremely narrow view which can only explain this abstention on the score of bankruptcy and business incapacity.

Active Persecution of Puritans   129

But there is still the matter of the imprisonment to deal with, and without a clear knowledge of the facts of the case the hard way of poverty seems to have ended in the shame of the debtor's prison.

Early in 1587 an action was raised against John Shakespeare by one Nicholas Lane.[1] The matter arose from a dispute regarding a transaction which took place in June 1586. Henry Shakespeare of Snitterfield owed a sum of £22 to Lane, and it was asserted that in conference with the parties John Shakespeare had promised to make himself responsible to Nicholas Lane for a sum of £10, in the event of his brother Henry Shakespeare failing to pay the amount owing. On Michaelmas Day 1586, the day on which the sum was due, Henry Shakespeare failed to discharge the debt, and consequently Lane claimed the money from John Shakespeare, as the alleged surety for his brother. This liability was denied, and Lane apparently fell back upon the security of the sponging-house, and had John Shakespeare arrested and flung into prison, for on March 29th a writ of *habeas corpus* was issued,—" Johannes Shakesper protulit

[1] See Appendix *C*.

breve dominae reginae de habeas corpus cum causa coram domina regina r. in curia prox. post XVIII Pascoe,"—in order that plaintiff and defendant might fight out the matter in open Court.

The action lasted over five months, and was contested every step of the way by John Shakespeare, and, so far as we have been able to trace, it is by no means clear that Lane proved his contention and won the case. But be the end what it may, it proves John Shakespeare's financial stability rather than his poverty. He was put into prison because he had money to meet Lane's claim, not because he was penniless, for the plaintiff, who had all the circumstances before him, must have known John Shakespeare's position to be a satisfactory one, or he would not have accepted him as security, and he would not afterwards have claimed the debt unless he had knowledge that it could easily have been paid him. It is absurd to think that Nicholas Lane would have taken the word of, and proceeded against, a broken man. And, on the other hand, John Shakespeare proves his ability to afford what must have been considerable law expenses in defending himself from what he evidently considered to be an imposition. The writ of *habeas corpus* was the means whereby he was freed from the confinement of the sponging-house in order that he might fight the question of his liability in open Court. Lane wanted his money, not his incarceration, for a word to the Ecclesiastical Commissioners would have been far more effective in the way of securing imprisonment. By his action he makes it clear that John Shakespeare could have discharged the debt had he been so inclined, and the whole transaction is a telling argument against the destitution theory. It is poor reasoning to say that because a man is accepted as security, and afterwards proceeded against for the recovery of a brother's debt, that therefore that man must have been a bankrupt.

V

Marked down as a Puritan Recusant

CHAPTER V

MARKED DOWN AS A PURITAN RECUSANT

THE year 1586 is a notable one for all Shakespeareans. It marked the close of the official career of Alderman John Shakespeare the father, and the opening of the much greater career of his son, for, according to common assent, William Shakespeare left Stratford about this time to try his fortune in London. The too readily accepted gossip of a century later says that he left home under circumstances of poverty and shame.

According to Rowe (1709), nimble fingers and a bitter tongue made him powerful enemies in Sir Thomas Lucy and the Laws, and he was consequently obliged to shelter himself in London. " By a misfortune common enough to young fellows he had fallen into ill company, and amongst them some that made a frequent practice of deer-stealing;

he engaged with them more than once in robbing a park that belonged to Sir Thomas Lucy of Charlecote, near Stratford; for this he was prosecuted by that gentleman, as he thought, somewhat too severely, and in order to revenge that ill-usage he made a ballad upon him, and though this, probably the first essay of his poetry, be lost, yet it is said to be so very bitter that it redoubled the prosecution against him to that degree that he was obliged to leave his business and family in Warwickshire for some time and shelter himself in London."

In 1708 a worthy archdeacon named Davies had given even stronger testimony than that repeated by Rowe. According to him, Shakespeare was given "to all unluckinesse in stealing venison and rabbits, particularly from Sir Thomas Lucy, who had him oft whipped and sometimes imprisoned." Here the archdeacon enables us to test the veracity of the statement he makes, for, on questions of whipping and imprisonments, one Court Record of the time is worth more than the word of even a bench of bishops of one hundred years later; but there has never been the slightest documentary

Marked down as a Puritan Recusant 137

evidence of a conviction recorded against William Shakespeare, nor does anything appear in any contemporary Stratford Records against the man who in less than fourteen years after he left home became one of the leading inhabitants of the borough, owner of the best house in it, leaseholder of the tithes of three important parishes, one who entertained preachers of the gospel at his own house when they came to do Sunday duty, whose minister was the famous Puritan, Dr. Richard Byfield, and whose favourite daughter Susannah married one of the best known religious enthusiasts in Warwickshire. Success and prominence have always had their detractors, and in a small country town surely some envious busybody would have unearthed the fact of these "oft whippings and imprisonments" and flung them as a stone at William Shakespeare. That there was bitter feeling between William Shakespeare and Sir Thomas Lucy there is no doubt, but the clearest intimation of its existence is to be found in the well-known passages of the poet's own writings. Shakespeare himself reveals to us its strength and bitterness, and Sir Thomas Lucy to the end of time will have to bear the sting of his lashing satire. But the animus is not that of the man who has been justly punished for a drunken or a thievish freak, nor does the successful man in the days of his prosperity care to revive in his native village stories of well-deserved punishments and imprisonments. A wise man would let the dead past bury its dead, and Sir Thomas Lucy would have been left alone. But Shakespeare did neither,—he pilloried his enemy, and made him the laughing-stock of the world. There can be no two opinions regarding the heinousness of deer-stealing, and without doubt Sir Thomas Lucy could have punished Shakespeare severely had he been brought before him.

But there is another side to the question, and one which has played a prominent part in days of religious coercion, when deer destruction was as common as the houghing and maiming of cattle in these later days of political coercion. It was a common act of revenge or retribution.

In 1556, Queen Mary's Chancellor, Heath, had his deer destroyed by men who hated him for religious intolerance; the High Constable of Lancashire had his deer crippled by Papists in

Marked down as a Puritan Recusant 139

1600. Outrages of a like nature were continually occurring in times of popular excitement and party feeling. It is no unlikely thing that a high-spirited youth, driven to recklessness by the harsh treatment of his father under heavy Recusancy Laws by a renegade justice of the peace, may have taken this step in reprisal. If John Shakespeare was feeling the severity of the Ecclesiastical Uniformity Laws as administered by Lucy (the man who had hobnobbed with a Puritan Council when Puritan feeling was high in England and much was expected from the Queen), there must have been vengeful feelings against the traitorous justice, and young men might easily let their feelings carry them to the extent of deer destruction. Justice Shallow threatens to make a Council matter of it, a Star Chamber business; but Parson Evans says: "It is not meet the Council hear of a riot, there is no fear of God in a riot." Professor Dowden, in his admirable little book on William Shakespeare, mentions a presumed cause for the animosity of Lucy : " It has been suggested that he may have felt some animosity against the Shakespeare family as possibly having sympathy with the old religion, for

Sir Thomas Lucy was not only a game-preserver, but also a zealous Protestant."

Here Professor Dowden assumes that the Shakespeares were Roman Catholic, and Sir Thomas Lucy a Puritan, forgetful that the term "zealous Protestant" is too loose for the time of which it is used, for both Prelatist and Puritan would claim the title, and also that Sir Thomas Lucy, if a "zealous" Puritan, would not be likely to be the head of the Commission whose chief duty was to hunt down the Puritans. A great deal depends upon a correct understanding of Sir Thomas Lucy's position, for many commentators, following an absurd mistake of Malone, have taken for granted that Lucy was a Puritan. He was a man zealous for religion, and may have begun as a Puritan, but certainly the evidence of his later days points to a vigorous Prelatism. He was knighted by Elizabeth in 1565 after he had entertained her at Charlecote on her way to Kenilworth. In 1586 he was one of the nobles and gentlemen appointed to escort Mary of Scots from Tutbury to Fotheringay.

In 1571 he was returned to Parliament, and took an important part in the religious discussions of the

Marked down as a Puritan Recusant 141

House, being appointed upon Committees which had for their object reforms in the Church. In 1572, the year when the Puritans were gathering all their forces, Mr. William Devereux and Mr. Clement Throckmorton were elected; and on the death of the first named, Sir John Huband was chosen in his place. In 1584, when the Acts of Uniformity were being more vigorously enforced, Sir Thomas is again returned to Parliament, and at once shows his zeal in matters ecclesiastical by being appointed to present a petition to the House of Lords respecting the "liberty of godly preachers" (*D'Ewes' Journal*).

Malone, on the basis of these facts, dubs Lucy a Puritan, and does so in the following brilliant piece of historical criticism: "He appears to have taken an active part in the House of Commons in several matters of importance, and to have been one of that Puritanical party who about the middle of the Queen's reign, while they resisted some unwarrantable extensions of prerogative, began to broach those republican doctrines, and to attempt those innovations which, at a subsequent period, after having been duly matured in the detestable school of Geneva, contributed under the management of a band of wicked and artful hypocrites to destroy at once the Church, the Nobility, and even the Monarchy itself."

After which Malone hastens to pick up his besmirched Sir Thomas Lucy by saying "but he was sturdily attached to his Sovereign."

Again quoting from *D'Ewes' Journals*, page 355, in reference to the case of Dr. Parry of Queenborough, Malone gives us another example of his keen and logical insight.

Under date of Tuesday, Febuary 23rd, 1584, the Journal records—

"Upon a motion began by Sir Thomas Lucy and continued by Sir Thomas Moore, 'that those of this House which are of Her Majesty's Privy Council, may in the name of this whole House be humble suitors unto Her Majesty, that forasmuch as that villainous traitor Parry was a member of this House in the time of some of his most horrible and traitorous conspiracies and attempts against Her Majesty's most royal person (whom Almighty God long preserve), Her Majesty would vouchsafe to give Licence to this House, for *that many are of*

Marked down as a Puritan Recusant 143

the fellowship of this Association, to proceed to the devising and making of some law for his execution after his conviction, as may be thought fittest for his so extraordinary and horrible treason.'"

The language is a trifle ambiguous, but the object of both mover and seconder is clear enough. Sir Thomas Lucy was seeking a stringent law to deal with members of Parliament who like Parry might be persuaded by cunning Jesuits to join them in the numerous conspiracies against the life of the Queen. Already Coligny had perished in Paris in 1572, William the Silent had been shot down with poisoned bullets by Gerard in Delft, 1584, numerous seminary priests and Jesuits were inciting fanatics against an excommunicated Queen, and the plots which resulted in John Savage's mission of assassination, and John Ballard's intrigue with Anthony Babington for the deposition and murder of Elizabeth, were more than set afoot.

The discovery of Parry's treachery revealed the disquieting truth that this widespread association of intrigue and assassination had its representatives in the very House of Commons itself, and therefore honest Sir Thomas Lucy, who was sturdily attached to his Sovereign, desired to see some enactment which would deal adequately with the danger. Surely if Malone had had one grain of pity for the unfortunate man who must for ever bear the weight of Shakespeare's scorn, he would not have added the utterly ridiculous line, " Sir Thomas Lucy was without doubt one of the Associators above mentioned."

Lucy was not on the best of terms with Leicester and the House of Warwick (well-known supporters of Puritanism), and in the chronicles of the Lucy family there is a statement which confirms this : " To please the Earl of Leicester, Shakespeare wrote the *Merry Wives of Windsor*, and took off Sir Thomas Lucy as Justice Shallow."

As is well known, in the first copy of the *Merry Wives* there is no mention of the dignities of Justice Shallow, and Falstaff appears under the name of Sir John Oldcastle, the well-known sufferer for conscience' sake in 1417, but in later editions, when James of Scotland, a Presbyterian, was next in succession to the throne, and active persecution had died away, Shakespeare makes amends for the light use of Oldcastle's name, and calls him a "valiant martyr and a virtuous peer." "Oldcastle died a martyr, and this is not the man." In November 1604 the *Merry Wives* was played before James I., and the full satire as it now appears was in the text. Some idea of the bitterness which prompted its insertion may be gained from the fact that at this time Sir Thomas Lucy had been dead for some four years. It is very clear that something deeper than a prosecution for a youthful escapade must have roused the antagonism in the mind of Shakespeare, and the most reasonable deduction is that his indignation was roused at the sight of his own father being harassed and hunted by persecuting justices, ever under the shadow of imprisonment and death and a mark for every vindictive spy and informer. There is more than one cry for vengeance against tyrannical justices of the period. Perhaps the most pathetic of all is that which was placed as an inscription on the coffin of Roger Rippon, a Puritan who died of gaol fever in Newgate, 1592.

"This is the corpse of Roger Rippon, a servant of Christ, and Her Majesty's faithful subject, who is the last of sixteen or seventeen which that great enemy of God, the Archbishop of Canterbury, with his High Commissioners, have murdered in Newgate within these five years, manifestly for the testimony of Jesus Christ. His soul is now with the Lord, and his blood crieth for speedy vengeance against that great enemy of the Saints and against Mr. Richard Young, a justice of the peace in London, who in this and many like points hath abused his power for the upholding of the Romish Antichrist, Prelacy and Priesthood."

But even if the deer-destroying incident never happened, it is not absolutely necessary to presuppose folly or crime because a young man of twenty-two leaves a country town like Stratford and makes a bid for fortune in the metropolis. The road to London has always been a well-worn one, and Stratford was in the direct line. If we take the immediate friends of the Shakespeares, we find that as a rule one representative of the various families after his education was finished set out for London.

Adrian Quyney, John Sadler, Henry Field, each had sons in London. Young Quyney built up an independence for himself. Richard Field, as a young printer, turned out William Shakespeare's first literary venture; and Greene, another Stratford youth, was a member of a London company of actors.

John Sadler the younger became a grocer in Bucklersbury, and when fortune smiled upon him, with Richard Quyney, "as gentlemen and citizens of London," he gave £150 to be lent out, the interest of the fund to be given to the poor of Stratford for ever (see the Bequest); but when he left home he started out with nothing more than a horse to ride on and enough money to buy food on the journey. "He joined himself to a carrier and came to London, where he had never been before, and sold his horse in Smithfield; and having no acquaintance in London to assist him, he went from street to street and house to house asking if they wanted an apprentice, and though he met with many discouraging scorns and a thousand denials, he went on until he light on a Mr. Brokesbank, a grocer in Bucklersbury, who though he long denied him for want of sureties for his fidelity and because the money he had (but ten pounds) was so disproportionable to what he used to receive with apprentices, yet upon his discreet account he gave of himself and the motives which put him on that course, he ventured to receive him on trial, in which he so approved himself that he accepted him into his service, to which he bound him for eight years."

No one feels called upon to invent discreditable reasons for the departure of these young companions of William Shakespeare from Stratford. The proceeding is a perfectly natural one, and therefore needs no explanation. Why, then, is it necessary to assume in the case of the greatest genius of them all that drunkenness and knavery were the compelling causes of his sojourn in London? The argument is based upon the idea that drunkenness and knavish recklessness alone account for the destruction of a justice's deer, and one can easily understand how the stories of whippings and imprisonments and reckless drinking bouts came to be handed down by Betterton, Rowe, Davies, and other pickers-up of ill-considered trifles on the basis of the bitter satire upon Lucy in the *Merry Wives of Windsor*; and it is not difficult to perceive how readily men, whom it may fairly be supposed were not authorities on the religious struggles of Elizabeth's day, would light upon a very commonplace and everyday explanation for an exploit which involved the destruction of deer. It may have been clear to the mind of William Shakespeare that any chance of a successful career in Stratford was practically closed to him while the fearfully repressive measures were being put in force against Puritans, and when every suspected household lived in hourly dread of confiscation and imprisonment, and he may have determined, like Greene, Quyney, Sadler, and other young men of his acquaintance, to make an attempt to push his fortunes in London; but so far as one can judge from the testimony of his own pen, this resolve was more quickly realised by the hasty act and extreme measure into which religious intolerance and a bitter contempt for the persecuting Sir Thomas Lucy had hurried him. In any case, when the storm of persecution had blown over, he had no fear in returning to Stratford; he occupied a most honourable position in it; not a whisper was breathed against him on the score of youthful wickednesses; and if he had not himself recorded the incident in his own play, it is questionable if the world would ever have heard the story of his "unluckinesse in stealing venison and rabbits, particularly from Sir Thomas Lucy, who had him oft whipped and sometimes imprisoned." That his departure was a wise step there can be no doubt, for there was a grave danger attending any manifestation of Puritan feeling. The activity of Whitgift's Commissioners had increased tenfold, and it soon became a difficulty to provide prison accommodation for the numberless Puritans arrested. From 1586 to the time of the coming of the Spanish Armada the Ecclesiastical Courts were in almost daily session.

In one respect the sailing of the Fleet caused the tide of religious persecution to be stayed. Men of all conditions forgot that they were Papist, Puritan, or Prelatist in remembering that they were Englishmen, and volunteers from every county and every church flocked to the Queen's standard to man the ships or trail the pike. Success crowned their efforts, and the flag of Spain sank, with hundreds of doomed vessels, into the depths of its greatest humiliation, and all England breathed freely. The united stand against the Armada

Marked down as a Puritan Recusant 151

touched the hearts of all except the clerical advocates of persecution, and in 1592, when the Whitgift Tests were once more cramming the prisons, a stream of petitions from the counties flowed in against the tyrannies of the High Commission.

Parliament was preparing to take up the question when a peremptory message from the Queen directed "that the House might redress such popular grievances as were complained of in their several counties, but should leave all matters of State to herself and her Council, and all matters relating to the Church to herself and the Bishops."

Mr. Attorney Morrice, Puritan Chancellor of the Duchy of Lancaster, nothing daunted by this grave menace to constitutional freedom, and supported by Francis Knollys and Oliver St. John, moved "that the House do enquire into the proceedings of the Bishops in their spiritual Courts" (Heylin, Strype, D'Ewes, 474).

He was arrested almost immediately in the precincts of the House by order of the Queen, deprived of office, dismissed his profession, and committed a close prisoner to Tutbury Castle. The next day Elizabeth sent a message to the House wherein she expressed her will as follows:—

That it was wholly in her power to call, determine, assent or dissent to anything done in Parliament.

That they were not to meddle with matters of State or causes ecclesiastical, and that she wondered that they should attempt such a thing, and grievously offend her.

And finally, that it was her Royal pleasure that no Bill touching any matters of State and causes ecclesiastical should be there exhibited.

Then came the discovery of Hackett's mad treason, and in the consequent excitement Parliament proceeded to pass one of the severest and most disgraceful Acts that ever sullied the Statute Book of England. It gave full rein to fanatical cruelty, and was merciless in its extreme severity.

It was entitled "An act for the punishment of persons obstinately refusing to come to Church and persuading others to impugn the Queen's authority in Ecclesiastical causes."

It was directed against Puritan nonconformity, and

Marked down as a Puritan Recusant 153

it was meant to most effectually prevent the straying away of Puritans from their parish churches. It conferred upon the Commissioners powers of perpetual imprisonment, perpetual banishment, and death without benefit of clergy (this latter privilege one which even the vilest felon might claim).

"If any person above the age of 16 shall obstinately refuse to repair to some Church, Chapel, or usual place of Common Prayer to hear Divine Service, for the space of one month, without lawful cause, or shall dissuade any of her Majesty's subjects from coming to Church to hear Divine Service or receive the Communion according as the Law directs, or shall be present at any unlawful assembly, conventicle or meeting under colour or pretence of any exercise of religion, that every person so offending and lawfully convicted shall be committed to prison without bail till they shall conform and yield themselves to come to Church and make written declaration of their conformity.

"But in case the offenders against the Statute being lawfully convict shall not submit and sign the declaration within three months then they shall adjure the realm and go into perpetual banishment.

And if they do not depart within the time limited by the Quarter Sessions or Justices of the Peace, or if they return at any time afterwards without the Queen's Licence, they shall suffer death without benefit of clergy."

This and other statutes would have led to a revolution if all their provisions had been carried out in the spirit which created them, but fortunately sympathy was aroused everywhere for the threatened Recusants, and numbers were quietly shielded by conforming neighbours and townsmen. "'Tis hard to get witnesses against the Puritans," wrote one ecclesiastic, "because most of the parish favour them, and therefore will not appear against them." But the anxious life of the Nonconformists may be easily appreciated when we consider the tremendous forces arrayed against them, and the sufferers of the time have made their sorrows re-echo even to this day. "Their manner of pursueing and apprehending us is with no less violence and outrage, their pursuevants with their assistants break into our houses at all times of the night and break open, ransack and rifle at their pleasure."

In a petition to Parliament a prisoner writes:—

Marked down as a Puritan Recusant 155

"Some of us had not one penny about us when we were sent to prison, nor anything to procure a maintenance for ourselves and families but our handy labour and trades, by which not only we ourselves but our families and children are undone and starved. Their unbridled slander, their lawless privy searches, their violent breaking open houses, their taking away whatever they think meet, and their barbarous usage of women and children we are forced to omit lest we be tedious.

"That which we crave for us all, is the liberty to die openly or live openly in the land of our nativity; if we deserve death, let us not be closely murdered, yea starved to death with hunger and cold, and stifled in loathsome dungeons."

These are but typical cases, and the death records of the persecutions only add their testimony to the black business. It was the Queen's supreme effort to root out the Puritanism she hated. Much capital for Roman Catholicism has been made out by some writers in connection with these statutes, and it has been taken for granted that the poor and ever-faithful Romanist was the chief sufferer by the Elizabethan persecutions.

He suffered terribly, it is true, and had to bear the weight of the malice of Puritan and Prelatist, but he was hated more for his subserviency to intriguing and traitorous Rome than for his religion. The Queen's sympathies ran more in his direction than in that of the Puritan, and after the crushing defeat of the Armada and Elizabeth's diplomatic triumphs all along the line, his secret worship was not so much the object of the attack of the Ecclesiastical Courts as that of the Protestant Nonconformist. Elizabeth looked upon Roman Catholicism as loyalty to the Pope, a State religion in many parts of Europe which she could understand, but Protestant nonconformity she considered rebellion against herself, a new assertion of individual rights of conscience which meant unfailing antagonism to her own claims of ecclesiastical supremacy. Malone's description of the Puritan movement may be adopted as expressing the view of Elizabeth. "Matured in tne detestable school of Geneva, it contributed under the management of a band of wicked and artful hypocrites to destroy at once the Church, the Nobility, and even the Monarchy itself."

Marked down as a Puritan Recusant 157

Elizabeth was a strong-willed sovereign, and she entered with all the pride of her strength into the conflict with the Puritan, little dreaming that in spite of every tyranny his principles would finally win the battle, and that the divine right of liberty of conscience would sweep its way through prison and death, as a few years later the axe shore through her own fondly-cherished delusion of the divine right of kings. Hence the true phase of the conflict must be borne in mind in discussing these later persecutions of Elizabeth, and it must not be forgotten that these statutes were directed mainly against the Puritan.

In Warwickshire, Cartwright of Warwick was arrested in 1590 and released two years later. Humphrey Fenn of Coventry had been often cited before the Courts. John Udall, who in 1586 had been deprived for Puritanism, but restored through the influence of the Countess of Warwick, had been tried and sentenced for his alleged connection with the Martin Marprelate Tracts, and died a prisoner in the Marshalsea Prison in 1592.

John Hales of Coventry, Robert Wigston of

Woolston, and Job Throgmorton of Haseley were suspects, on account of the secret printing press which was causing so much excitement through the land, for it is significant of the strength of the Warwickshire Puritanism that the Marprelate Tracts were printed at three places in the county, and all within a short distance of the town of Stratford.

The bitterness aroused against the hidden railers was such that inquisition was made in every county, and most diligent search failed to discover the whereabouts of the press, but, as is well known, it was proved to have been working at White Friars in Coventry, the residence of John Hales, at Woolston, Robert Wigston's house, and Haseley, the residence of Job Throgmorton; and even after its seizure at Manchester, the controversy was continued by Throgmorton, first by another press at Haseley, and finally by one worked by Waldegrave, Penry, and Throgmorton from the Puritan centres of Edinburgh and Rochelle.

John Shakespeare seems to have been keeping himself in the background during all these years.

Marked down as a Puritan Recusant 159

He was taking part in some public duties, but they were only such as serving on juries and witnessing wills. Twice in 1591 he served as a juryman, and in 1592 we find him engaged in two instances in making inventories of the goods of deceased persons, a task which, according to old law books, must only be performed by trustworthy and credible men.

With regard to his position as a property owner, the Exchequer Court Returns furnish reliable data. In 1590 he was returned as holding the Henley Street property, and his possession of it is still further attested in the fact that in 1597 he sold a strip of the land to George Badger, his neighbour, and about the same time another strip of the same property to one named Willis, a piece of land "conteyninge seventene footes square, that is to say, seventene footes everye way." These sales are interesting as proving that the Henley Street property, at least, never passed out of the possession of John Shakespeare until his son William succeeded him as heir, and they have also a bearing on the "poverty theory" of his life, for here without doubt we have *bonâ-fide* sales of property, business transactions in which John Shakespeare is making a fairly good bargain although lessening the amount of his real estate. A pathetic picture might be drawn of the poor old man, weary with the confinement of the debtor's prison, parting with his strips of land in order to scrape together a little money, for they are certainly more powerful evidences of poverty than the Snitterfield and Asbies transactions, if the selling of a possession is to be accounted a proof of destitution. But the year in which this transaction took place, namely, 1597, is one in which no one can assert destitution for the old man, because his son William had returned to Stratford a wealthy man, having bought the well-known residence at New Place; his granaries, when corn was at famine prices, were well-stocked with grain, and he was about to purchase the important tithe leases of Stratford, Old Stratford, Bishopton, and Welcombe for the very considerable sum of £440.

In 1592 Sir Thomas Lucy, Sir Fulke Greville (the elder), and other justices of the peace had been appointed under the Recusancy Act of

Marked down as a Puritan Recusant 161

that year, to make diligent inquiry as to the monthly attendances at the parish churches, because, as will be remembered, the Act was especially concerned with the enforcing of attendance. "Anyone over sixteen years of age who shall refuse for the space of one month without lawful cause, shall be committed to prison without bail till they shall conform and yield themselves to come to Church and make written declaration of their conformity." Officers and spies of the Ecclesiastical Courts had the districts under supervision, and regular reports were obliged to be submitted. Many well-known persons refused to attend the services of the parish church, many pleaded old age and sickness, and some made fear of process their excuse. As a rule the officials inquired into each case, and the justices added the testimony of their seals or signatures to the reports sent up to the Court.

The well-known document, which is signed and attested on every page by Sir Thomas Lucy, is as follows :—

"The seconde Certificat of the Commissioners for the Countie of Warwicke touching all such persons as either have bene presented to them, or have bene otherwise fownde owt by the endevoire of the sayd Commissioners, to be Jhesuites, seminarye preestes, fugitives, or recusants within the sayd Countie of Warwick, or vehementlye suspected to be sutche, together with a true note of so manye of them as are alreadye indicted for thear obstinate and wilfull persisting in their recusancye; sett down at Warwicke the xxvth day of September in the 34th yere of her Majesty's most happy raigne and sent upp to the lordshipps of her Majesty's most honourable Privye Councell.

"The names of sutch recusantes as have bene heartofore presented for not comminge monethlie to the Churche according to her Majesty's laws and yet are thoughte to forbeare the Church for debtt and for feare of processe, or for some other worse faultes, or for age, sickness or impotencye of bodie."

Then follows a long list of names, concluding with fifteen concerning which explanatory notes are given. Nine come not to church for fear of process for debt. Six are kept back

Marked down as a Puritan Recusant 163

by age or infirmity. The list of nine is as we enumerate:—

> " Mr. John Wheeler.
> John Wheeler his soon.
> Mr. John Shackspere.
> Mr Nicholas Barneshurste.
> Thomas James alias Gyles.
> William Bainton.
> Richard Harrington.
> William Fluellan.
> George Bardolfe.

It is said that these laste nine coom not to Churche for fear of process for debtte.

> Mistress Geffreyes, vid.
> Mris Barber.
> Julian Coorte.
> Gryffen ap Roberts.
> Joane Welche.
> Mris Wheeler.

Weare all here presented for recusantes, and doo soo all so continewe saving Mris Wheeler who is conformed, and Gryffen ap Roberts, now deide.

But the presenters say that all or most of theese cannot come to the Churche for age or other infirmities."

The section upon which the names appear is that devoted to Puritan Recusants, not to that occupied by Jhesuites, seminarye preestes, fugitives, and Papists.

The names are those of persons who were forbearing attendance at their parish church, and who unless they could show a lawful excuse would be imprisoned as nonconforming Puritans. Such terms would not, and could not be used of the Roman Catholics. Papists were persecuted for being Papists, not for forbearing attendance at the parish church. The names quoted are considered by the presenters to be *bonâ-fide* members of the Established Church who are breaking the law which insisted on a monthly attendance at Church services, and the excuses tendered might possibly have been of service to a non-attending Puritan, but would not have been accepted for one moment from a Papist.

That the explanation concerning the fear of process for debt was no more than an excuse is

Marked down as a Puritan Recusant 165

apparent from the fact that there is no record of such processes being in force against any of the individuals, and also that among the names are those of three men and the wife of another who have held office as Aldermen and Bailiff of Stratford.

Mr John Wheler and his son are keeping away for fear of debt, but Mrs Wheler, in a later return, even after her conformity in the second return, as recorded above, is given as persisting in her absence from church, " Johne Wheyllers wyffe in Henlie Streytte."

Mr John Wheler, as we have seen, was twice Bailiff of Stratford; he was always a man of property, and to the end of his life is recorded as possessing lands and houses. His association with Alderman John Shakespeare in all matters of Puritan reform we have already traced. Mistress Barber was the wife of Thomas Barber, who was several times Bailiff of Stratford, in 1586 and again in 1594, that is, two years after his wife has been returned as a Recusant. He was borough chamberlain with Nicholas Barneshurst, whom we have seen in 1572 deputed to deliver the sum of £VI to Adrian Quiney and John Shakespeare when they were appointed to arrange matters in London touching the affairs of the town and the commonwealth, before the assembling of the Puritan Parliament.

In all movements of Puritan energy in Stratford we have had a certain number of names recurring, Shakespeare, Wheler, Barber, Barneshurste, Quiney; it is not astonishing, therefore, when Puritan extinction is being aimed at that we should discover the names on a return sent up to the Privy Council as persistent forbearers from Church.

That John Shakespeare was not forbearing church for fear of process for debt is clearly shown by the Court of Record returns. He was one of the most litigious of men, but he has no cases whatever from 1591 to 1593. From July, 2 Phil. and Mary, to March, 37 Elizabeth, there are no less than 67 entries of cases in which his name appears on one side or the other, and some of his actions are with his best friends, as Adrian Quiney, Francis Herbage, Thomas Knight, and Roger Sadler; but in 1591 there is only one entry, and that is of a case wherein John Shakespeare sued as plaintiff in a debt recovery action and won with costs. Mr.

Marked down as a Puritan Recusant 167

Halliwell Phillipps says (Notes, 7th ed., p. 397): "The alleged suspicion so far as regards John Shakespeare was a mere device, this being abundantly clear from the fact that there was no action of any kind against him in the Court of Record throughout the year in question; and from the last day in June to the end of 1591 the only suit that affected him was one in which he was the plaintiff and recovered a debt with costs."

This Recusancy Certificate shows Sir Thomas Lucy to be an enthusiastic Queen's Churchman actively engaged in putting into force the stern enactments of Parliament. It also shows us that there was in the town of Stratford a group of those sturdy religionists who forbore attendance at the parish church because of conscientious objections to obnoxious doctrines and ceremonies, who preferred a mode of Protestant worship other than that enforced by the law, and were prepared to suffer hardship and imprisonment for the Crown Rights of King Jesus and for liberty of conscience. The significant incidents we have marked in the lives of John Shakespeare, John Wheler, Thomas Barber, and Nicholas Barneshurste fall naturally into line when viewed from their proper standpoint of Puritan earnestness, and the Recusancy Return is but the fitting climax to careers against which the laws represented by the return were promulgated. It was precisely for such men that the Act of 1592 was passed; it is no wonder, then, that it sufficed to bring them within sweep of the law. But there were also other good reasons for Puritan non-attendance at church beside the powerful plea of conscientious scruple, for at that very time one of the greatest Puritan preachers of the day was holding services only a few miles from Stratford.

Thomas Cartwright had been made Warden of the Leycester Hospital at Warwick. Sir Francis Walsingham sent him a hundred pounds to buy books, and his friends the Earls of Warwick and Leicester did all they could to make his position a safe one. His career had been a brilliant but stormy one. Froude calls his appearance at Court "the apparition of a man of genius." Beza said of him that "the sun doth not see a more learned man." In 1569 he had been made Lady Margaret Professor of Divinity in Cambridge, but because of his Puritanism he had been silenced and deprived.

He was the foremost controversialist of his day,—a fact amply attested by the judicious Hooker in his great work. After eleven years' exile in Antwerp he returned to England in 1585, but was arrested on landing by Bishop Aylmer "by Her Majesty's commandment." After a short imprisonment he was released, and found shelter in Warwickshire. The Leycester Hospital was exempt from Episcopal jurisdiction, and Cartwright could preach there without a bishop's licence and in defiance of all ecclesiastical deprivation. Here he attracted to his able ministry the earnest men for many miles around; it is recorded "that there was not a nobleman or gentleman of quality in all the country that looked heavenward or was of any account for religious learning but sought his company." In addition to his duties, he preached every Sunday at 7 a.m., and frequently in the afternoons, and when it was known he was to hold a service, grave men ran like boys to get a place in the church. It is certain that Puritans who were dissatisfied with the meagre and unspiritual services of their parish churches would be sure to flock to Warwick to hear Cartwright, for as

Humphrey Fenn wrote: " If persons would hear a sermon they must go, in some places, five, seven, twelve, yea, in some counties twenty miles, and at the same time be fined twelve pence a Sabbath for being absent from their own parish church, though it be proved they were hearing a sermon elsewhere."

This was before the final enactment of 1592, but it is not at all unlikely that before the terribly severe Recusancy Act became the law of the land, John Shakespeare, John Wheler, Adrian Quiney, Thomas Barber, Nicholas Barneshurste, and other well-known Stratford men might have been seen Sunday after Sunday wending their way along the pleasant country lanes which lie between the town and Warwick, to listen to the eloquence of a man who was one of the ripest scholars in England and the foremost Presbyterian Puritan of his day.

VI

William Shakespeare and Puritan Influences

CHAPTER VI

WILLIAM SHAKESPEARE AND PURITAN INFLUENCES

AFTER two years of the Recusancy Act the persecution of Puritans relaxed somewhat, and cases of prosecution were transferred from the jurisdiction of the spiritual courts to be dealt with by the common law of the land in the temporal courts. This was a great privilege, but a still more valuable one was given in 1598, when the Puritans were allowed to remove their causes from local and Episcopal jurisdiction to Westminster Hall. There was what seemed to be a worldly wisdom in this toleration, for James of Scotland, presumably a strong Presbyterian, was acknowledged to be the successor of the aged Elizabeth, and he had more than once interceded on behalf of the persecuted Puritans. "From this time until the Queen's death there was a kind of cessation of arms between the Church and the Puritans; the combatants were out of breath, or willing to wait for better times. Some apprehended that the Puritans were vanquished, and their numbers lessened by the severe execution of the penal laws. But the true reason was this: the Queen was advanced in years, and could not live long in the course of nature, and the next heir to the Crown being a Puritan (James VI. of Scotland), the bishops were cautious of acting against a party for whom His Majesty had declared, not knowing what revenge he might take when he was fixed on the throne; and the Puritans were quiet, in hopes of great matters to be done for them upon the expected change."

The storm had passed over the land although the clouds had not disappeared. In the sunshine Prelatist and Puritan began once more to harry the unfortunate Papist. With the passing of the tempest renewed prosperity came into the life of John Shakespeare, and the old man, now about sixty-four years of age, entered upon the last stage of life under circumstances which seemed to

Shakespeare and Puritan Influences 175

promise rest and quietness. His own affairs were prosperous enough, and in any case the rapidly accumulating wealth of his son removed him from any fear of change of fortune. In 1597 William Shakespeare bought the house in New Place, and engaged in numerous business transactions in the neighbourhood of Stratford, and at the request of a number of his friends invested some £440 in the purchase of the tithe leases of Stratford, Bishopton, and Welcombe. In view of the oft-asserted Roman Catholicism of the Shakespeares, this purchase of the tithe leases is noteworthy. Would a Papist have been allowed to invest his money in this way? And if allowed by the Prelatist and Puritan opponents, would the Roman Catholic Church have held him guiltless in thus trafficking in sacred things? for in the eyes of devoted Papists this was spoliation with a vengeance. William Shakespeare may doubtless be a great gain to their Church in Roman Catholic eyes, but surely the heroism of Papists during the long dark years of Elizabeth is something far better and nobler. The Romish Church records are full of splendid examples of heroism for conscience' sake during these truly awful times; hedges, byways, secret chambers, dungeons and martyrdoms, bore witness to the devoted constancy of members of the old Faith. But what can be said of the claimed Roman Catholicism of the Shakespeares? It was a disgrace to the annals of the Church of Rome, and it is a very wide charity indeed which, after a knowledge of the undeniable acts which they committed in antagonism to Papistry, still claims to number them among the Faithful. If John Shakespeare was a Roman Catholic, he was a dishonest hypocrite of the worst type, and one whom it is exceedingly difficult to believe could have continued so long to hold the affections of the Stratford people. In the face of his official and private acts and undoubted leadership among his fellow-townsmen, it is incomprehensible how anyone could dub him Papist. It is only on the lines of Puritanism that his career becomes intelligible and inspiring and all the facts of his life seem to marshal themselves in proper order, and show him to be a man of sterling honesty and integrity, a sufferer for conscience' sake, and one who would dare every risk of

Shakespeare and Puritan Influences

imprisonment and death rather than be coerced into what he considered ceremonialism and dishonesty.

In 1596 John Shakespeare applied a second time for a grant of arms, and is described as a justice of peace, "and was Bayliffe Officer and Cheffe of the town of Stratford uppo Avon xv or xvj years past. That he hathe landes and tenements, of good wealth and substance £500. That he married a daughter and heyre of Arden a gentleman of worship"; and at the bottom of the grant (Herald Off. MSS.) there is a note: "This John sheweth a patent thereof under Clarence Cook's hands in paper xx years past."

In 1596 Henry Shakespeare of Snitterfield died. In the next year we have the last record of transactions in land, when, as before stated, John Shakespeare sold strips of his Henley Street property to his neighbours, Willis and Badger, and then all record of the father's life seemed to be merged in the greater career of his son.

In 1601 the end came, and from the town which had seen so much of his happiness, activity, and suffering the soul of John Shakespeare passed beyond the shadows into peace. He was buried on September 8th, aged seventy, and about seven years afterwards, almost to the very day, September 9th, 1608, was followed by his true love and gentle consort Mary Arden, whom he had wooed and won in the leafy lanes of Warwickshire beside the sweet banks of the swiftly flowing Avon.

They have passed into that silent land where the strifes and differences which separate men are resolved into their true significance before the throne of the God of Love, and where Puritan, Prelatist, and Papist are no longer distinguishing battle-cries; but we are compelled to ask in the interests of historical truth questions as to the principles which animated and controlled John Shakespeare's life. From all we have adduced it is manifest that he could have been no Roman Catholic; his actions, associations, friends, offices, public career, as recorded in the Town Records, all negative the idea of his being of the old Faith, and his persecutions equally show that he was no Prelatist. What was he, then? What was that man who first came to the front in the strongly Protestant first years of Elizabeth; who super-

Shakespeare and Puritan Influences 179

intended the alterations of the Town Chapel, defacing images, destroying sacred pictures and tearing down crosses and rood-lofts; who as chief magistrate was especially active in the suppression of a Roman Catholic rising and the persecution of Robert Perrot; who with Adrian Quiney cleared away the Romish vestments, and with the same friend represented the interests of Stratford when the Puritan Parliament of 1572 was assembling; who refused to participate in a levy which had for its object the repression of Puritans, allowing his name to be published as a defaulter; who trained his household in the nurture and admonition of the Lord so excellently that his son stands unrivalled in literature for his power of biblical quotation; who was the lifelong friend of John Wheler, Thomas Barber, and Nicholas Barneshurste, men identified with him in Puritan movements and coupled with him in Puritan Recusancy returns?

What was the religion of the man whose business capacities carried him into the front rank of his townsmen when Puritanism was tolerated and Roman Catholicism terribly persecuted, but whose career became a continual struggle when the iron hand of intolerance was laid upon the Puritan?

The stream of evidence runs consistently in one direction and leads to one conclusion, and that is, that John Shakespeare was one of those stalwart Protestants who took their theology from the school which produced a Calvin, a Knox, a Tyndale, and a Cartwright, and was of those who under the name of Puritan contributed to one of the most glorious pages of England's history.

We turn now to a consideration of the influences of the home life of William Shakespeare, in order to trace if possible the secret of his powers as a biblical student, and to seek indications of the precise nature of the home in which he was trained.

That his early surroundings were eminently religious we cannot doubt. Shakespeare is the poet of humanity because he strikes the deepest notes of human nature, but he strikes them as a man of intense religious feeling; he is above all a teacher of true righteousness, and beneath the light laughter of the Elizabethan poet there is always the deep earnestness of the Hebrew prophet.

Shakespeare and Puritan Influences 181

Biographers present divergent views according to their own theories. Halliwell Phillipps writes: "The poet was educated under the Protestant direction, or he would not have been educated at all. But there is no doubt that John Shakespeare nourished all the while a latent attachment to the old religion, and although like most unconverted conformists of ordinary discretion who were exposed to the inquisitorial tactics of the authorities, he may have attempted to conceal his views even from the members of his own household, yet however determinately he may have refrained from giving them expression it generally happens in such cases that a wave from the religious spirit of a parent will imperceptibly reach the hearts of the children and exercise more or less influence on their perceptions."

Knight says: "With the great Bible before her, the mother would read aloud to her little ones the beautiful stories of the Bible."

"We believe that the education of William Shakespeare was grounded upon the Book, and that if this Book had been sealed to his childhood he might have been the poet of Nature and of passion; his humour might have been as rich as we find it and his wit as pointed, but he would not have been the poet of the most profound as well as the most tolerant philosophy; his insight into the nature of man, his meanness and his grandeur, his weakness and his strength, would not have been what it is."

Once again quoting from Halliwell Phillipps: "Fortunately for us the youthful dramatist had, excepting in the schoolroom, little opportunity of studying any but a grander volume, the Infinite book of Nature, the pages of which were ready to be unfolded to him in the lane and field, amongst the copses of Snitterfield, by the side of the river or of his uncle's hedgerows." It is true that the Infinite book of Nature might have taught William Shakespeare how to become an expert poacher or deer-stealer, but it is difficult to perceive how it would help him to quote *ipsissima verba* from Holy Scripture without the aid of a grander volume.

From 1570 to 1572 Walter Roche was headmaster of Stratford School. He was followed, 1572 to 1577, by Thomas Hunt, afterwards deprived curate of Luddington, who died in 1612, four years

Shakespeare and Puritan Influences

before his old pupil, but not before he had seen him become one of the most prominent citizens of the borough. He was appointed to the school in 1572, the year when Adrian Quiney was bailiff and John Shakspeare was chief alderman, about the time when the Romish vestments were cleared away. He was suspended for open contumacy on September 2nd, 1584. William Shakespeare was under his care from the age of eight to that of thirteen.

In 1577 Thomas Jenkins was appointed, and held office until 1580, when he was succeeded by John Cotton; hence in the most susceptible periods of his childhood William Shakespeare was under the tuition of two lifelong friends of his father,— Walter Roche, appointed when the prosecution of Robert Perrot had just been carried through by John Shakespeare and the Papal Excommunication had been launched against England, and Thomas Hunt, curate of Luddington. Children usually went to the Grammar School about six, or, at latest, seven years of age. It seems certain that both at home and at school William Shakespeare came under strongly Puritan influences.

Which Bible would be put into his hands, from

the pages of which he would learn the words and phrases afterwards used so freely by him in his writings? Was it the "Great Bible," as indicated by Knight, or the Puritan Bible, as evidenced by Mr. Halliwell Phillipps? for, despite the "Infinite book of Nature," he does give Shakespeare the Genevan Bible. The first complete Bible published in England was that of Coverdale in 1535, but the edition was disposed of with some difficulty. It was followed by the Great Bible, or Cranmer's, in 1540; yet here again the prejudice against a vernacular Bible was so great that a number of injunctions and even penal laws were required to force it into circulation. Henry VIII. issued a proclamation regarding it, and the Vicar-General ordered "that one book of the whole Bible of the largest volume in English should be set up in some convenient place within the churches, that the parishioners might commodiously resort to the same and read it."

In 1557 Whittinghame revised Tyndale's New Testament, but it was not until 1560 that the book which became in the widest sense the household Bible of the nation was introduced from Geneva.

Shakespeare and Puritan Influences 185

The Queen, after some changes, granted a seven years' patent for printing it in England. It was published in a handy quarto size, in Roman type instead of black letter, and divided into chapter and verse. Afterwards the Common Prayers and Psalms were printed with it.

It had a wonderful circulation, and was eagerly bought up in all the Puritan households throughout the country; chapmen hawked them, traders carried them to and fro, and even in remote farmhouses and solitary cottages the Word of God was earnestly studied. Of eighty-five editions of the Bible published during the reign of Elizabeth, no less than sixty were of the Genevan Version.

In 1568 Archbishop Parker superintended the production of what is known as the Bishops' Bible; it was intended to supersede the Genevan, and did so in the public services of the Church, but it never displaced the Genevan in private use, and "we find that the Puritans who held so many livings in the Church of England, often in defiance of all authority, took their texts from the Breeches Bible."

In 1582 the New Testament was translated by the Roman Catholics at Rheims.

In 1609 what is known as the Douai Bible was published from the English Roman Catholic "College of Doway the Octaves of al Sainctes 1609."

William Shakespeare was a child of two years when the Genevan Bible was published, of ten when the Bishops' Bible was sent down, and a man of over fifty when the Douai came from France. It is difficult to see how a Roman Catholic English version could in any way have contributed to the wonderful biblical knowledge of the poet, or any Bible, however great, which was not in the fullest sense of the word a household Bible.

Roman Catholic piety has never been a piety founded primarily upon the Word of God; there are certain distinguishing marks which always differentiate the Papist from the Puritan ideals of righteousness. Dante and Shakespeare may be taken as examples of the different methods of training. Shakespeare draws all his religion from the Bible, Dante from the literature of Roman Catholicism, such as books of devotion, the Fathers, and traditionary sources. Free thinker though he was in many ways, and shaken loose from many

Shakespeare and Puritan Influences 187

of the binding superstitions of his day, Dante never released himself from his earliest training. His great poem from first to last breathes the life of Mediæval Catholicism, and from it the theology, fancies, theories, and beliefs of the Romish Church might be built up into a system, even though every other manual were destroyed. Despite his criticism of some of the popes, Dante was never placed in the list of proscribed authors, and, to quote the words of a Roman Catholic writer, "the *Divina Commedia* remains substantially a magnificent exposition of the Catholic faith, and has thus been studied and extolled by theologians and popes."

In order to illustrate the point more fully, the words of Father Bowden of the Oratory, in his preface to Dr. Franz Hettinger's *Divina Commedia* (Burns & Oates, 1887), may be quoted: "Though the poet knows no guide but the Church and her teachers, he by no means disparages reason. The idea in its development embraces the whole circle of Catholic theology. In politics, philosophy, and theology, Dante is essentially Catholic and orthodox."

"The structure of Heaven is determined by the

Shakespeare: Puritan and Recusant

nine orders of angels, as described by the Fathers and Schoolmen. From Holy Scripture, from theology, from the revelations of the Saints, Dante thus drew his most precious materials, and constantly *employs the Church's liturgy and office as their most fitting expression.*" This last phrase as underlined exactly illustrates the point of difference between the Papist and the Puritan, between Dante and Shakespeare. When the well-trained Roman Catholic desired to illustrate or intensify his meaning, the words of the Church's liturgy and office immediately presented themselves as the fittest vehicle of expression. When the Puritan desired the same result, instinctively and with like readiness the words of the Bible sprang up in his mind. In both Dante and Shakespeare we have the result of a systematic and careful training in earliest youth, the one on strictly Roman Catholic lines and the other on strictly Puritan. Whatever Shakespeare may have been in his manhood, there can be no doubt as to the careful religious and Puritan training of his childhood, and it is instructive to note that he never entirely broke away from Puritan surroundings and influences. His father's friends became his associates and kinsmen,—the Whelers, Quineys, Sadlers, Barbers and Sturleys. With his house in New Place a pew was appropriated to him in the Chapel, and the famous Dr. Byfield and his no less famous sons became his minister and friends. Richard Byfield was minister of Stratford in 1596, and Nicholas Byfield, the well-known Puritan commentator, and Adoniram Byfield, the fighting Chaplain of the Parliamentary Army and one of the secretaries of the Westminster Assembly of Divines, were young men of Stratford.

When ministers came to visit or relieve Dr. Byfield, hospitality was offered them at New Place, and they made their temporary home with William Shakespeare. It was something to entertain a minister of the Gospel in those days; and one can imagine the astonishment of the worthy Dr. Byfield and his fanatical kinsmen if they had been told that they were sending their ministerial friends to a Roman Catholic household. The Puritans of the days of Elizabeth had not the abhorrence of the stage which the corruptions of Charles II.'s reign called forth, and they could quarter a minister of the

Gospel in the house of an actor and dramatist with a good conscience, but they drew the line at a Papist's.

Again, the favourite daughter of Shakespeare was married to Mr. John Hall, M.A., a medical man, who was perhaps as well known for his religion as for his medicine.

Led astray by a sentence in the preface of a book by a certain James Cooke, some supporters of the Roman Catholic theory have made John Hall a Papist; the phrase is, "nay such as hated him for his religion often made use of him." It occurs in a book entitled "*Select observations on English bodies*, first written in Latine by Mr. John Hall, Physician, living at Stratford upon Avon in Warwickshire where he was very famous. Now put into English for common benefit by James Cooke 1657."

"The learned author" says James Cooke, "lived in our time in great fame for his skill far and near. Those who seemed highly to esteem him and whom by God's blessing he wrought these cures upon, you shall find to be among others, persons noble, rich and learned. And this I take to be a great signe of his ability that such who spare not for cost, and they who have more than ordinary understanding, nay such as hated him for his religion often made use of him."

He was employed by the Northumberland family, the Warwicks, Leycesters, Comptons, Northamptons, and several of the High Church and Roman Catholic aristocracy; he was the friend and associate of the well-known Puritan divines John Trapp and Thomas Wilson, and when the latter was vicar of Stratford, John Hall was made churchwarden in 1628 and sidesman in the next year. The vicar and his Puritan associates discussed religious affairs at New Place, and the Vicarial Courts were occasionally held there. When Rev. Thomas Wilson was accused of holding conventicles, John Hall was one of his most vigorous supporters. A thanksgiving prayer after a severe illness is well worth recording as an indication of the piety of the man to whom William Shakespeare intrusted his favourite daughter Susannah as wife.

"Thou, O Lord, which hast the power of life and death and drawest from the gates of death, I confesse without any art or counsell of man but only from Thy goodnesse and clemency Thou hast saved me from the bitter and deadly symptoms of a deadly fever, beyond the expectation of all about me, restoring me as it were from the very jaws of death to former health, for which I praise Thy name, O most Merciful God and Father of our Lord Jesus Christ, praying Thee to give me a most thankfull heart for this great favour, for which I have cause to admire Thee."

Susannah Hall, as her epitaph testified, was also noted for her piety. William Shakespeare at New Place was thus in a deeply religious atmosphere, and those who were nearest to him and dwellers under his own roof were conspicuous for their devotion to Puritan worship. It is not likely that a Roman Catholic in Elizabeth's day would receive Puritan ministers into his house, attend the ministry of a Puritan like Dr. Byfield, and marry his daughter to John Hall. It may be urged that Shakespeare was a man of wide charity and marvellous intellectual outlook, and possibly so great in his sympathies that he could see the good points and enjoy the fellowship of Puritans, even although he himself belonged to the persecuted

Shakespeare and Puritan Influences

Church of Rome, but the same could not be urged in favour of Hall, Trapp, Byfield, and Wilson, for it would be a miracle of toleration to find them seeking the friendship of Papists. However easy it might have been for Shakespeare, it would have been impossible for them.

Again, the wording of Shakespeare's will is worth a little notice, for there was a Puritan and a Papist method of phrasing a will, and many men took the opportunity of declaring their faith in this manner. Humphrey Fenn of Coventry and numerous sufferers for conscience' sake did so. Robert Arden's will, made in the reign of Philip and Mary, runs: "Fyrste I bequethe my solle to Allmightie God and to our blesside Ladye Sent Marye and to all the holye companye of heven."

A Puritan's will usually began as Shakespeare's did: "First, I commend my soule unto the handes of God my Creator, hoping and assuredlie believing that through thonelie merits of Jesus Christe my Saviour to be made partaker of lyfe everlasting."

The internal evidences of Shakespeare's works as pointing to his Protestantism form a separate field, but it is not out of place to mention one or two facts which seem to bear upon his Puritanism: his eulogies of Henry of Navarre, the Huguenot leader: his use of a very well-known Puritan book published in 1603, Harsnett's *Declaration of egregious Popish Impostures*, from which he has collected most of the names and allusions he puts into the mouths of Lear and Edgar respecting the demons of the earth and storm: and a passage from the *Taming of the Shrew*, Act iii. sc. 1, 60–80:—

"*Hortensio*—Madam, before you touch the instrument,
　　　　　To learn the order of my fingering,
　　　　　I must begin with rudiments of art ;
　　　　　To teach you gamut in a briefer sort,
　　　　　More pleasant, pithy, and effectual,
　　　　　Than hath been taught by any of my trade :
　　　　　And there it is in writing fairly drawn."

And then follows, Ut, Re, Mi, fa, Sol, la, etc.

The sense of this passage is taken almost literally from the page which prefaces the Psalms in the Genevan Bible and Prayer Book, where Sternhold and Hopkins give their setting of some of Marot's ballad tunes.

"Thou shalt understand, gentle Reader, that I have (for the helpe of those that are desirous to

Shakespeare and Puritan Influences 195

learn to sing) caused a new print of note to be made with letters to be joyned to everye note: whereby thou maiest know how to call everie note by his right name, so that with a verie little diligence thou mayest the more easilie by the viewing of these letters, come to the knowledge of perfect solfaying whereby thou mayest sing the Psalms more easilee and readily. The letters be these, Ut, Re, My, fa, Sol, la."

Concerning the question of the version of the Bible used by Shakespeare, the question can only be positively settled by a careful comparison of the earliest folios with the various Bibles, so that the exact quotations may be identified and localised. This is a task calling for much patient research and careful study, which would amply repay any earnest investigator. So far as we have been able to follow in this direction, we have, under the guidance of a booklet by Halliwell Phillipps, found enough to justify us in saying that our views concerning the Puritan upbringing of the poet receive rather striking corroboration. Many of the passages quoted by Shakespeare are found only in the Genevan Version, and cannot be traced in any other Bible,—for instance, the well-known text in Jeremiah xiii. 23, "Can the Ethiopian change his skin or the leopard his spots?" Shakespeare says:

> "Lions make leopards tame;
> Yea, but not change their spots;"

evidently based upon the text. Coverdale, Matthew, the Bishops', the Great Bible, as well as Cranmer's, render the passage, "Can the Man of Inde change his skin and the cat of the mountayne her spottes?"

The Genevan is the only version which speaks of the animal as the leopard: "Can the blacke moor change his skin, or the leopard his spots?"

In *Henry IV.*, Part I., Shakespeare says, referring to the Prodigal in Luke xv. 16, "from eating draff and huskes."

The word "huskes" is not found in Coverdale, Matthew's, Cranmer's, the Bishops', nor the Great Bible, but in the Genevan the passage runs: "And he would fain have filled his belly with the husks the swine ate."

Shakespeare, with the Genevan, writes "Iscariot"; the other versions have "Iscarioth."

Shakespeare and Puritan Influences 197

In the *Merchant of Venice* the strategy of the patriarch Jacob is instanced in the passage:—

> "That all the earlings which were streaked and pied
> Should fall to Jacob's share,
> The skilful shepherd peeled me certain wands,
> And stuck them up before the fulsome ewes,
> Who when conceiving, did in eaning time
> Fall parti-coloured lambs."

The words used by the versions is "ring-straked"; the Genevan alone uses the term particoloured: "They brought forth yong of particolor and with great and small spots."

Many other instances are quoted and compared by Mr. Phillipps in his little book, *The Version Shakespeare used*, and in the preface he writes the following important opinions, especially interesting to us in the light of the Puritanism which we have endeavoured to show is undoubtedly in the public acts of John Shakespeare, and perhaps entitled to more weight because the writer of them seemed to favour the theory of the Roman Catholicism of the Shakespeares.

"The contents of the following pages will it is thought tend to the impression that the Version of the Bible usually read by Shakespeare was that known as the Genevan. That Version first appeared in the year 1560, and was the one chiefly read in family circles during the youth of the great dramatist."

Appendices

A.—ON SHAKESPEARE'S BIBLICAL KNOWLEDGE[1]

MR. F. J. FURNIVALL, summarising from Bishop Wordsworth, says:—

"No Book is so often quoted or alluded to by Shakspere as the Bible. Not only does he mention 'Holy Writ' four times, 'Scripture' three times, 'the Word' three times, 'the Book of Life' once, 'the Book' nine times, and 'it is written' once; not only does he quote Bible passages in his plays; not only has he references to 'Pilate washing his hands, to 'sacrificing Abel's blood,' to the Psalmist, to the Prodigal Son, to Jacob grazing his Uncle Laban's sheep, to 'Lazarus and Dives that lived in purple,' and to Abraham's bosom; not only does he mention Adam twenty-two times, Eve six times, Cain six times, Abel, Noah, and Job twice, Christ nine times, Jesus sixteen times; but he accepts, or makes his characters accept, the whole 'scheme of salvation' set forth in the Jewish and Christian Testaments, and the stories of the Apocrypha too. 'From the Creation to the general Doom' Shakspere, dramatically at least, takes the Bible's word as to the beginning, the life, and the end of the heavens, the earth, and man. He has angels good and bad, Satan and

[1] *See page* 37.

the devils; Paradise and the state of innocency, with Adam digging his garden, the serpent tempting Eve, the fall of man, the curse of the Serpent, Abel's murder by Cain, Noah's flood, Job's poverty, Jacob's staff, Pharaoh's dreams, the plagues of Egypt, the manna in the wilderness, a law from the Book of Numbers, the sword of Deborah, Jephtha's love for his daughter, Samson's temptation and carrying away of the town gates, Goliath, Nebuchadnezzar, Daniel.

"From the New Testament, Shakespeare gives us the slaughter of the Innocents, the Gadarene swine, the Last Supper, Judas's kissing and betrayal, Pilate's washing his hands and delivering Christ to be crucified, the robber Barabbas, Christ's words on the Cross, 'they know not what they do,' the field of Golgotha, and the sepulchre of the Lord.' In the speeches of certain of the characters the whole 'scheme of salvation' is unhesitatingly accepted. Paradise and the Fall, the doctrine of Original Sin, Miracles, the need of the sacrifice of Christ's life to work the atonement between God and man, 'to free us from His Father's wrathful curse'; the Resurrection and the Judgment, the Hell, the Heaven, etc.; Immortality of the Just, the efficacy of prayer."

B.—ON WRITS OF DISTRAINT [1]

PROCEDURE by "Distringas" was one of the commonest methods in the monthly Court of Record, and nearly every business man in Stratford had been proceeded against in this way. It carries no weight in deciding for or against a man's financial position. Writs of distraint were as common as business greetings even among well-tried friends. We cite a few instances from the Court Records:—

May 6th, 1558.

"Adrianus Quyny et Thomas Knyght petunt distringas versus Johannem Shakspeyr in placito debiti."

[1] *See page* 32.

Appendices

June 5th, 1558.

"Willielmus Malpas ad hunc diem petit distringas versus Johannem Shakespere in placito debiti pro vIIJs.

June 9th, 1585.

"Fiat distringas versus Thomam Lytleton."

A month after this—

"W. Parsons *v.* Thomas Lytleton—accio continuatur."

June 20th, 1588.

"Johannes Shaxpere queritur versus Johannem Tomson in placito debiti."

April 1589.

"Johannes Shakespere queritur versus Willielmum Grene de placito debiti."

October 22nd, 1589.

"Johannes Shaxpere queritur versus Ricardum Sutton in placito debiti."

November 5th, 1589.

"Fiat distringas versus Johannem Tomson ad sectam Johannis Shaxpere in placito debiti."

"Fiat distringas versus Ricardum Sutton ad sectam Johannis Shaxpere in placito debiti."

October 26th, 1586.

"Johannes Hathawaie queritur versus Thomam Hathawaie in placito debiti : distringas."

On February 1st, 1587, three months after the writ is issued,

"Johannes Hatheway et Thomas Hatheway concordate sunt."

The 1586 distraint issued against John Shakespeare was led up to in the following way :—

On October 27th, 1585, John Brown takes action.

"Item, Johannes [Browne] queritur versus Johannem Shakesper defendentem de placito debiti "

The case was a disputed one. In November a writ was applied for and obtained.

November 10*th*, 1585.

"Fiat distringas versus Johannem Shaxpeare."

Fourteen days later a second writ was applied for.

November 24*th*, 1585.

"Fiat alias distringas versus Johannem Shaxpere ad sectam Johannis Browne in placito debiti."

Why was this second writ needed? On January 19th the sheriff's officers returned the writ of distraint "because the aforesaid John Shakespere has nothing that can be distrained upon, therefore an order of capias may be made against the same John Shakespere."

January 19*th*, 28 *Eliz.* 1586.

"Ad hunc diem servientes ad clavam burgi predicti retornavit preceptum de distringas eis directum versus Johannem Shackspere ad sectam Johannis Browne, quod predictus Johannes Shackspere nihil habet unde distringere potest. Ideo fiat capias versus eundem Johannem Shackspere ad sectam predicti Johannis Browne, si petatur."

February 16*th*, 1586.

"Fiat capias versus Johannem Shaxspere ad sectam Johannis Browne in placito debiti."

This "capias" seems to be the next step in this disputed case, for Shakespeare seems somehow or other to have evaded the operations of the writs of distraint; because he is a penniless man, say the poverty theorists, having no property he could not be distrained upon. But he had landed property, as the Exchequer Returns show.

However, a "fiat capias" was granted, but he somehow managed to evade its operations, and on March 2nd, 1586, another "capias" was applied for.

"Fiat alias capias versus Johannem Shaxspere ad sectam Johannis Browne in placito debiti."

After this there is no further record either of "concordate sunt" or of drawing a pen through the name, as in the case of the Quiney writ of 1558 for £6, but the case was probably settled in due form, for three months afterwards, July 20th, 1586, John Shakespeare was summoned and served as a juryman in an important case.

C.—ON NICHOLAS LANE'S ACTION [1]

Stratford Court of Record,
January 18th, 29 *Eliz.* 1587.

"Johannes Shaxpere attachiatus fuit per servientes ad clavam ibidem ad respondendum Nicolas Lane in placito transgressionis super casum."

February 29th, 1587.

"Nicolaus Lane narrat versus Johannem Shaxpere in placito transgressionis super casum, et defendens, licentia loquendi (?)."

March 1st, 29 *Eliz.* 1587.

"Johannes Shakesper per Willielmum Courte venit &c. et dicit quod non assumpsit prefato Nicolas Lane, modo et forma prout predictus Nicholaus eum narrat."

March 29th, 1587.

"Johannes Shakesper protulit breve domine Regine de habeas corpus cum causa coram domina Regina.

"Mercurio proximo post xviij Pasce."

[1] *See page* 129.

Index

	PAGE
ANATHEMA of Rome	62, 63
Arden, Agnes	95
Arden, Mary	15, 33, 36, 95, 177, 178, 181
Arden, Robert	16, 93, 101, 193
Arguments based on chamberlain's accounts	26, 28, 35
BIBLE (Douai)	39, 186
Bible (Genevan)	184, 194 *et seq.*
Bible Versions	184
Biblical quotation	36 *et seq.* and Appendix
Biblical reference in *Taming of the Shrew*	194
Bonner's Inquisition	17
Book by John Hall	190
Byfields, The	189, 192
CALF-KILLING legend	17
Carlyle on Shakespeare	14
Cartwright, Thomas	22, 112, 124, 168, 180
Chamberlain's accounts	25, 28
Close of John Shakespeare's civic career	125
Collections for the poor	46
Council enactments (attendance)	19, 58
Coventry Puritans	21
DANTE and Shakespeare	186
Death of Agnes Arden	95
Death of Henry Shakespeare	128
Death of John Shakespeare	176
Death of Robert Arden	16

Index

	PAGE
Death of Udall	157
Debtors' Prison	129
Deer destruction	138
Demolition of Popish symbols	26, 27, 28
Distraint writs	29, 31, 124, and Appendix
Douai Bible	39, 186
Dugdale's Record of Old Chapel	26
Duplicity of the Lambarts	103
ELIZABETH and Puritanism	65, 85, 119
Enactments to compel uniformity,	52, 54, 76, 84, 87, 119, 122, 152, 161, 174
Enthusiasm for Elizabeth	64, 112, 150
Excommunication of Elizabeth	61, 62
FROUDE on Cartwright	168
Froude on Whitgift	87
GENEVAN Bible	184, 194 *et seq.*
Gossip concerning William Shakespeare	136
HALL, John	190 *et seq.*
Halliwell Phillipps	30, 33, 97, 114, 167, 181, 182, 197
Harsnett's *Popish Impostures*	194
How property was protected	95, 97 *et seq.*
LANE'S prosecution	129
Lansdowne MSS.	95
Lease by Agnes Arden	95
Local reference in *Taming of the Shrew*	107
Lucy and Malone	144
Lucy and Shakespeare	137, 145
Lucy, Sir Thomas	66, 116, 136, 140, 145, 161
MALONE mistaken	144
Malone on Lucy	144
Malone on Puritanism	141
Mary Arden	15, 33, 36, 95, 177, 178, 181
Mary of Scotland	55, 140
Marprelate Tracts	158
NORTHUMBERLAND rising	54
OATH "officio mero"	120

Index

	PAGE
PERROT, Robert	19, 56, 60, 73
Phillipps, Halliwell, quotations from,	30, 33, 97, 114, 167, 181, 182, 197
Pope insults Elizabeth	20, 61
Popish Impostures	194
Poverty theory of John Shakespeare's life,	29, 90, 98 *et seq.*, 129
Prayer by John Hall	190
Properties in Wilmcote and Snitterfield	16, 95, 97 *et seq.*
Property in Henley Street	15, 78, 159
Property of John Shakespeare,	16, 93, 78, 90, 97 *et seq.*, 159, 160, 177
Prosecution by Nicholas Lane	129
Protection of property	95, 97 *et seq.*
Puritan influences upon William Shakespeare	175, 189
Puritan zeal in Coventry	21
Puritanism (alleged) of Lucy	66, 140 *et seq.*
Puritanism of John Shakespeare—	
Bible training at home	38, 45, 186
Ministers and schoolmasters	78, 182, 189, 191
Prosecution of Perrot	19 *et seq.*
Protection of estates	96, 101 *et seq.*
Puritan Parliament of 1572	68
Recusancy Return	162
Refusal to attend Council	127
Refusal to pay levy	114
Remarks on proofs of Puritanism,	71, 72, 88, 115, 128, 167, 175, 178 *et seq.*
Sale of vestments	70
School and Chapel alterations	26 *et seq.*
Puritanism of Spenser, Milton, and Bunyan	85, 79
Puritans in prison	155
Puritans in Warwickshire	22, 59, 69, 112, 116, 137, 157, 162, 169, 179, 183, 189, 192
RECUSANCY Return	162
Reformer of Elizabethan days	89
Relics burned	21
Rising in Northumberland	54
Rome and the Bible	38–45, 54, 186
Rood-loft destroyed	28
SADLER'S journey to London	147
Schoolmasters of William Shakespeare	78, 182, 183
Shakespeare, Henry	128, 129, 177

Index

	PAGE
Shakespeare, John—	
Close of civic career	125
His appointments	17, 25, 31, 47, 55, 68, 73, 125
His character	27, 45, 57, 71, 72, 88, 176
His death	176
His difficulty with Lane	129
His political activity	68
His possessions. (See Property.)	
His religion. (See Puritanism.)	
His trade	16
Remarks on his life,	71, 72, 88, 115, 128, 167, 175, 178 *et seq.*
Shakespeare, Mary	15, 33, 36, 95, 177, 178, 181
Shakespeare, William—	
Associates	189
Bible knowledge	38, 45, 181, 186 *et seq.*, 195
Education	33, 181, 186
Puritan influences	175, 189
Quarrel with Lucy	137, 145
Schoolmasters	78, 182, 183
Wealth	160
Stratford accounts	25, 28, 46
Stratford appointments	17, 25, 31, 47, 55, 68, 73, 125
Stratford incorporated	13
Stratford opinion	34, 35
Spanish Armada	150
Spenser	85, 79
Test Articles of Whitgift	119
Udall's death	157
Uniformity enactments,	52, 54, 76, 84, 87, 119, 122, 152, 161, 174
Writs of distraint	29, 31, 124, and Appendix